couples who cope

Sustaining Love in Difficult Times

Jane P. Ives

DISCIPLESHIP RESOURCES

NASHVILLE, TENNESSEE

www.discipleshipresources.org

Other Caring Couples Network® Resources

Caring Couples Network (CCN) Handbook, by Richard and Joan Hunt (1996). This handbook provides basic information on organizing a CCN Team to minister effectively with couples and families.

Couples Who Care, by Jane P. Ives (1997). This collection of nineteen true stories illustrates dramatically how married couples can help other couples build enduring, fulfilling marriages.

Growing In Faith, United in Love, by Barb Nardi Kurtz (1998). This book offers material to help couples explore and develop important aspects of their relationships on their own, in six weekly sessions, or during a retreat.

Marriage: Claiming God's Promises, by Nan Zoller and Jack Gilbert (1998). This resource provides material for an eight-week study or for use in retreat settings to help couples nurture their marriages.

To order, call Discipleship Resources (800-685-4370). For more information, contact Office of Family and Life Span Ministries, Discipleship Ministries Unit, General Board of Discipleship, United Methodist Church, 1908 Grand Ave., Nashville, TN 37212-2129. Phone: 615-340-7170.

Cover and book design by Sharon Anderson

ISBN 0-88177-247-X

Library of Congress Card Catalog No. 98-70468

DR247

Contents

Preface and Acknowledgments

Since the 1997 publication of my first book, *Couples Who Care,* a collection of true stories illustrating effective marriage ministries, many new marriage ministry resources have appeared on the market. Promotional materials indicate an increased expectation that churches should exercise leadership in strengthening marriage and family life. Most marriage ministry programs focus either on preparing for marriage or on strengthening good marriages, in order to help couples experience increased fulfillment in their relationships.

But what about couples going through particularly troubled times? The stories in *Couples Who Cope* offer hope and suggest helpful strategies for couples facing challenging situations, whether caused by circumstances over which they have no control or resulting from their own choices. These stories also present insights and information to help churches minister more effectively to couples dealing with similar circumstances.

I want to express my deepest respect for and gratitude to those who shared their stories with me for this project. For those who chose to remain anonymous, names and some identifying details have been changed. In spite of the obvious pain involved in recalling these events, contributors report that telling their stories allowed them to affirm the growth and healing they have experienced and to realize the possibility of helping others by their witness. These stories, as well as those I could not use because of space limitations, strengthen my conviction that in marriage, as in our individual lives, hard times often provide our best opportunities for growth.

I also want to thank those who so richly bless my life and encourage my own personal and spiritual growth:

- my beloved husband, for your patience, encouragement, and helpful suggestions;
- our adult children and their mates, for the rich experiences you bring to our journey;
- our grandchildren, for the inexpressible joy bestowed by your love and exuberance;
- our colleagues in ministry, particularly those with whom we share in prayer covenants, study settings, and missional service.

This book is dedicated to the memory of my dear friend, Arlene Hamilton, whose husband contributed the concluding story in this book.
May you be blessed, dear readers, as I have been by this project.

Jane P. Ives

Introduction

Brides and grooms, standing before the altar making solemn vows "to love and to cherish until we are parted by death," may have given little real thought to the challenges that might lie ahead. Like poetry, the words roll off their tongues: "For better, for worse, for richer, for poorer, in sickness and in health." The realities to which these words point, however, demand commitment and skills that seem to have become increasingly scarce in our society. Even couples with the best of intentions may find themselves overwhelmed by unexpected circumstances and unable to sustain a loving relationship.

Happily, however, many couples triumph over separation, sickness, problems, and pain. Their relationships serve, like Noah's ark, to keep them afloat during high-water, troubled times. Some report even greater personal happiness, increased marital intimacy, and more-effective family functioning after coming through difficult experiences.

What is their secret? How do they claim the promise that "all things work together for good for those who love God" (Romans 8:28)? What inner resources, skills, and community support make the difference between those whose relationships fail under stress and those who come through hard times stronger in faith, in wisdom, and in their commitment to each other?

The following stories provide some answers to these questions. Grouped around themes (family crises and concerns, separation caused by career demands, relationship breakdown and recovery, illness of a spouse, and death), the stories explore common issues and illustrate how adversity may confirm particular strengths and/or surface aspects of relationships that need healing. These stories also illustrate the importance of communication and conflict-resolution skills that often make the difference between marriages that succeed and marriages that fail. These stories affirm that such skills can be learned and that we can indeed, with God's help, build enduring, fulfilling relationships and sustain love through even the most challenging situations.

Suggestions for Use

Individuals might use these stories to explore a variety of life circumstances and to learn how others have faced and grown through challenging experiences. Scripture passages and "Reflection" questions offer prompts for personal journaling and for deepening self-awareness. "Toolbox" pages present effective skills and principles for strengthening relationships.

Couples could read these stories aloud to each other, perhaps journaling separately in response to the questions and then dialoguing about what they have written.

Small groups could discuss the "Reflection" questions after reading the stories, either individually in preparation for the session or aloud within the group setting. These stories might also "prime the pump" for participants to share stories of their own or of people they know. The leader's guide (pages 103–15) provides additional activities and suggestions for group study, using either all the stories or selected sections only. Each story may be dealt with separately in approximately one-hour sessions, or they may be combined for longer group meetings or for retreat settings.

Marital-growth groups might allow time for couples to dialogue privately after individually recording their responses to the "Reflection" questions. In the larger group they could share, as they choose, new insights and learnings.

Clergy groups, lay pastoral care givers, Caring Couples Network® Teams, and others seeking to grow in their understanding of how to minister effectively to couples and families could use this resource as part of their continuing education.

The resource section (pages 118–20) describes other programs and materials for strengthening marriages and enhancing ministries to married couples.

Our Mutual Burdens Bear

Commentary

Harold Kushner, in his book *When Bad Things Happen to Good People* (page 133), reminds us that we have not been promised a life free of pain and disappointment. Even knowing that, few of us are fully prepared for hardships involving those we love most. The death of a child, sibling, or parent can trigger paralyzing grief. Caring for family members who are ill, injured, or in trouble demands not only increased amounts of a couple's time, energy, and ability to function smoothly as a team, but also considerable capacity for dealing with emotional stress. At such times, we want our mates to be competent in whatever ways the situation requires, as well as emotionally available to help us process our feelings.

In fact, families can be overwhelmed easily and need outside help, both to do the things that must be done and to heal the fear, anxiety, and frustration that usually accompany concern for loved ones.

In the following stories, you will see how couples have endured loss and traumatic experiences involving family members. You will also see how faith, loving relationships, and community support enable couples not only to cope but even to grow while caring for loved ones in difficult circumstances.

Do not, therefore, abandon that confidence of yours; it brings a great reward. For you need endurance, so that when you have done the will of God, you may receive what was promised.
HEBREWS 10:35-36

His Eye Is on the Sparrow

Our second child, Kara, was diagnosed at birth with a severe condition called Aperts Syndrome and died when she was twelve days old. John and I had just come through medical trauma with our first child, Janelle, who had been born two and a half years earlier, premature but healthy except for a heart defect. In the fall of Janelle's second year, the doctors recommended heart catheterization and open-heart surgery. When we went to Johns Hopkins in Baltimore, however, the staff there decided she was healthy enough to have a new "balloon" surgical procedure. The ninth child in this country to undergo pediatric heart angioplasty, Janelle came through beautifully. Our church friends, our colleagues at work, and our family all prayed for her and for us throughout. Afterward, we enjoyed a late but wonderful Thanksgiving celebration. A few weeks later, I realized I was pregnant. Kara was born in May, about two months premature. When we learned of her diagnosis, we were shocked, as there had been no indication of problems before her birth. I wondered if my exposure to x-rays during Janelle's treatments had been the cause. It is a terrible blow when you are preparing for life and death hits you smack in the face.

Again, our family and our church (an urban African American congregation) gave us wonderful support. I felt as though I had been hit by a truck and couldn't get up. My mother-in-law, who had experienced several miscarriages herself, helped me to see that these things happen and that you don't need to blame yourself for them. My father, a spiritual man, gave us guidance and shared his faith. Our pastor and church friends visited and prayed for and with us. Harold Kushner's book *When Bad Things Happen to Good People* also helped. In time, through faith, I was able to stand again. John seemed stronger than I throughout this experience. He even made arrangements for us to bring Kara home and care for her, but it was not to be.

Genetic counselors informed us that the chances of having a child with Aperts Syndrome were 1 in 113,000. It was hard to accept that there was no known cause. Losing Kara was especially difficult for me because many of my friends were expecting babies. People who thought we had a lot to offer as parents encouraged John and me to have children. The genetic counselors also encouraged us to try again, but warned us that what we had been through would put a strain on our marriage. Divorce rates are high for parents who lose a child, perhaps because they tend to blame each other. It never occurred to us to do that.

Two years later we were expecting again. This pregnancy was harder than anything else we had experienced, since we now knew firsthand what could happen. For months we walked on eggshells. Jocelyn was born several weeks early and, although my labor went quickly, I trembled throughout, not realizing how much emotion I had been holding in check. In spite of the pronouncement "Congratulations, you have a healthy seven-pound, eleven-ounce baby girl," I sent John to the nursery five times to make sure she hadn't been moved into the intensive care unit for newborns. When at last they brought her to me, I was terrified to open the blanket. John, who had been strong for me throughout the pregnancy, sat down and cried, partly in relief and partly in facing his pain at having lost Kara.

Some people take having a healthy child for granted, but we never did after the traumas we experienced. Eight years after Jocelyn's birth, Johnny was born slightly premature but healthy. We thank God every day for our good fortune. We have built our lives around our children and try to provide the best we can for them. When my father died a year after Johnny's birth, we rejoiced that he had lived long enough to know his grandson.

The following summer, while driving to Florida for a family reunion, our van flipped over and rolled down an incline near the border of South Carolina and Georgia. Our children were thrown out of the van, as this was before shoulder harnesses became standard equipment on vehicles. They seemed to be lying all over the highway. John was still strapped in the van, upside down, held against the crushed roof of the vehicle and unable to move because of two broken vertebrae in his neck. I was bleeding, and broken glass was everywhere; but somehow I wasn't frightened, just grateful to be alive and mobile. I felt an aura all around us, like the presence of guardian angels.

Some truckers stopped to help. Strangers comforted the children and stayed until the ambulance arrived. We were transported to a small hospital nearby, where Johnny and I stayed. John and the girls, Janelle with a broken leg and Jocelyn with breaks in both legs and her collarbone, were transported to a trauma center. I was frightened because it was difficult to get any information from the trauma center about John and the girls, but Johnny and I received wonderful care, both for our lacerations and for our troubled spirits. The nurses anointed me with oil and prayed while holding hands around my bed. They played with Johnny and made him laugh by putting feathers in his hair.

My mother, sisters, and brother, who had flown to Florida to meet us there, flew back to join us, rallying around to nurture and support us all. We stayed in Georgia for three weeks. When I was released from the hospital, I moved into a Ronald McDonald House, where family members helped care for Johnny until we sent him back to be with his paternal grandmother. When John and the girls flew home, in casts and braces, my brother-in-law drove me back because I was too terrified to get on a plane.

John was told he had only a five-percent chance of walking again, but some of his functions began to recover. He stayed in the hospital another three weeks, struggling to decide whether to have the injured vertebrae fused. One day after praying that God would let him know whether to have the operation, he dozed off and then awakened feeling better, confident that he would continue to improve without surgery.

Hospital staff evaluated our house and ordered hospital beds, medical equipment, and home-healthcare nurses. For the next three months neighbors and church folks brought in food and helped care for us all. John bought a new van, made reservations at Disney World for the Christmas and New Year holiday, and took seventeen members of the family there for a delayed vacation. Because the thought of driving terrified us, John hung a cross in the van and put Scripture verses in the automobile handbook. At first I kept screaming involuntarily when driving or riding in a car, but John told me that would have to stop. I turned my screams into praise affirmations, thanking God for his goodness and mercy. How blessed we are to have survived this accident without permanent injury to any of us.

I also know how fortunate we are to have grown up in religious families. John's family attended an integrated church, walking two or three miles to worship on Sunday, since the nearest black church was even farther away and they did not have a car. My father was a lay leader in The United Methodist Church, and was active both locally and at the conference level. Going to church and learning to live by faith in our daily lives prepared us to face these difficult experiences. Hymns, prayers, and Scripture gave us comfort and courage. Psalm 121, which we sometimes call the West Virginia Psalm because of its reference to the hills, holds special meaning for us.

With all that has happened, we continue to move ahead, confident that God is watching out for us. Some people get bitter and discouraged after experiencing such trauma, but we never have. Things happen, but it is what you do in response that matters. Now, even more than ever, we take nothing for granted and try to keep our priorities in order. People sometimes remark that we don't seem to let things upset us. Well, we have been through some biggies and are stronger than we ever were before. Day-to-day hassles seem trivial to us. Whatever happens, you have to hang in there and do the best you can.

These experiences changed our perspective and way of making decisions. We no longer postpone what we want to do, such as building a new home. Each day is a precious gift, and tomorrow is not guaranteed; so we jump at opportunities and do what we can as soon as we can. We are so grateful for our families' heritage of faith and for their modeling of faithful living. Marriage is not easy, and life's surprises can undermine a shaky relationship; but we have known God's presence in our most terrifying experiences, and we both can say with conviction, "His eye is on the sparrow, and I know he watches me."

KAREN AND JOHN WILLIAMS

John, director of the Jobs Training Project Act (JTPA) for his state, and Karen, coordinator of personnel for Kanawha County schools, live in Charleston, West Virginia.

Reflection

1. Who has modeled faithful living for you?

2. What traumatic experiences has your family (or another you know well) encountered?

3. When overwhelmed by events for which we are not prepared, how can others help us get back on our feet?

4. What attitudes and beliefs can help a couple facing tragedy to avoid blaming each other and keep their relationship intact?

5. How do you model faithful living for your children and others?

Likewise the Spirit helps us in our weakness; for we do not know how to pray as we ought, but that very Spirit intercedes with sighs too deep for words. And God, who searches the heart, knows what is the mind of the Spirit, because the Spirit intercedes for the saints according to the will of God.

Romans 8:26-27

choosing to Be Blessed

Our eldest daughter, Sarah, came down with pneumonia in December 1993, when she was nine years old. Since she had experienced some asthmatic bronchitis before, we saw no reason to worry. Ours was a pretty typical household, with three daughters, two harried parents, two jobs, a house never quite cleaned up, and meals seldom prepared ahead. We had just returned from a Thanksgiving holiday at Disney World and were ready to dive into Christmas decorating and shopping. After a week in the hospital, Sarah seemed ready to go back to school, but the doctor was concerned about her x-rays. She allowed Sarah to go home only on the condition that she not go out at all, and she arranged a January appointment for us at Duke University Medical Center. Because Sarah seemed so well, we considered all this an aggravation, rather than a cause for alarm.

Before the end of our first day at Duke, however, the doctors confirmed their suspicions that Sarah had cystic fibrosis. Robert and I were shocked and numbed by the news. The pediatric pulmonologist explained that since cystic fibrosis is a genetic disease caused by a recessive gene, both of us must be carriers. Therefore, our other two daughters, Lindsay and Laura, each had a twenty-five-percent chance of having the disease and would also need to be tested. Although this was not good news, the odds sounded hopeful, especially since both girls seemed healthy to us. The staff told us that the median life expectancy for children with cystic fibrosis was twenty-nine years at that time, but they hastened to add that new treatments and procedures, including transplants, should change that prognosis soon. They had seen life expectancy more than double during the last forty years. The gene for cystic fibrosis was not isolated until 1989, and new drugs and therapies have surfaced even during the last few years. The staff assured us gently, "Don't think you don't have to plan for college."

Rob and I, both in shock, didn't talk about our feelings. We headed home in a terrible snowstorm to pack for an extended stay and to get Lindsay and Laura. As soon as a bed became available in the pediatric unit, Sarah would receive a full assessment, including fat studies to determine pancreatic function; and we would be trained to care for her. Lindsay and Laura, six and three years old respectively, would be tested and, if necessary, admitted. We tried to be honest with Sarah about her disease and about these next steps. Finally, after a long silence, she asked, "Does this mean I'll have a shorter life?"

Rob replied firmly, "Not if we can help it. We'll give you the best care we can." We never did tell her a specific life expectancy. Already it's up to thirty-one, and we keep hoping new developments will increase that even more.

When we returned to Duke in January, we were so confident that one, if not both, of the other girls would be found disease-free that we arranged for their grandparents to pick up one or both after the testing. Even so—although we have always done what we are supposed to do—I really wanted to run away. Between the two trips to Duke, I was distracted and had a hard time focusing, so I had great difficulty deciding how much to pack for Lindsay and Laura.

At Duke again, sweat tests confirmed that both Laura and Lindsay had cystic fibrosis too. We stayed two weeks at the hospital learning to do their breathing treatments, which involve percussion therapy three times a day to keep their lungs clear, as well as using a nebulizer. We learned ways to keep track of their calorie intake, strategies for adding calories to their food, and what special vitamins they needed to take. I always knew I didn't want to be a nurse, but now I had to learn all these things in order to keep our girls alive. Rob was impressed when I corrected an intern who thought he had to draw blood one more time. I had kept track of what was done, so I knew better. Under all this pressure, Rob and I sometimes found ourselves sniping at each other, but he quickly reminded me that we were on the same team and needed to be supportive.

The days in the hospital were long and grueling, beginning before six in the morning so that Rob and I could shower and dress before starting the girls' first set of treatments. It was usually almost one the next morning before the last intravenous antibiotics had been administered. A never-ending parade of different medical personnel asked questions and taught us things; there was never a break. I don't know how we kept from collapsing, except that literally hundreds of people were praying for us all. One afternoon, when I should have been exhausted, I realized that not only was I not tired, but that I didn't even feel like I was walking from room to room. I was floating—or being transported—on prayers.

When we finally returned home late at night from Duke, with the girls all needing baths and treatments before they could go to bed, our spirits were buoyed by the welcome banner that greeted us, the helping hands of my mother, and the food that had been placed in our refrigerator. We got the girls up for school the next morning because we feared that if they had time to think about it too much, they might worry about how others would react. I talked to their teachers and drafted a letter to send to our friends to inform them of this new challenge in our lives. The doctors had told us we would have to decide whether to keep the girls' illness a secret or to share it openly. We decided to be open, partly because it is too difficult to keep something like this a secret, and partly because we didn't want the girls to feel they had a reason to be ashamed.

Although a woman in our church school class organized meals for us through the end of the school year, the schedule was still so crazy that for a while we just couldn't keep up with the new routines. The instructions for the equipment seemed like Greek to us, and we didn't have time to locate the less-expensive source for the girls' medications. When we returned for their checkups four and a half weeks later, we still had not unpacked from the January stay. A friend of mine who is a nurse offered to take time off to help us for a while. She came during spring break and pitched right in, focusing entirely on us and our needs. In addition to relating well to the girls, she interpreted instructions and took over a number of responsibilities.

The staff at Duke had assured us that our lives would get back to normal, or nearly so. They told us to keep the girls active because physical activity is critical to their long-term well-being. We immediately enrolled them in gymnastics, tennis, and dance classes and got them outside playing and riding their bikes. It isn't easy for the girls or us to find the two hours every morning and evening for their treatments, as well as everything else that needs to be done. In addition, we return to Duke every three months for reevaluation and checkups. Still, we try to focus on life, treating the disease as just something else we have to figure into our schedule.

One heartbreaking aspect of their diagnosis for me was the anticipation that they would never be able to participate in summer camp, as I had through Girl Scouts when I was growing up. This had been such an important part of my personal formation that I did not even dare pray for a way for my daughters to have that experience. Still, God answered my heart's longing when I discovered that a Girl Scout camp in a neighboring state offered support services in order to include girls with disabilities. Although cystic fibrosis is not a disability, the promise of such services led me to inquire. You can imagine my joy when I was assured that the girls' treatments would not be a problem and that the camp nursing staff included two people trained in percussion therapy and in the use of nebulizers.

I think there is a big difference between an acute problem and a chronic condition. With an acute problem, everyone gears up to help; then it is resolved and you get back to normal. With a chronic illness, you know it will never be resolved. I worry that people will tire of hearing us talk about the girls; and since they look healthy and are out and about and active, it's hard for others to comprehend what we are dealing with. Some people get uncomfortable hearing about our experience, partly because of their close relationship with the girls and the pain they feel for them, and partly because our experience scares them. A later review of the girls' earlier x-rays revealed signs of the disease that had not been recognized. If radiologists misread their x-rays, people realize, it could happen to them or their loved ones. When I finally began to tell my pastor about all that was happening, it was a tremendous relief to experience his understanding and willingness to let me spill it all out.

At first Rob and I had little time to think; we just divvied up the responsibilities and kept on going. There was so much to do that we didn't really get in touch with our grief until about a year later. As we began to process our grief, however, we realized that we would have to work at not letting this take over our whole relationship. We began to train baby sitters so that we could go out for dinner and a movie and focus on each other and our relationship. It would have helped if we had been able to have more private couple time early on to process our feelings and share with each other.

We deeply appreciated family and friends who volunteered to come in and lend a hand or to learn how to do the treatments so that they could give us release time. Having someone else around not only helps to get the treatments and other household tasks done, but it also encourages us to talk about other things and keeps us from being overwhelmed by the disease. Such support would have really helped during that initial training at the hospital, when we were completely overwhelmed by the number of people literally standing in line to consult with us. A support group also would have been good, as it always helps to be with others facing similar challenges. A woman whose son has cystic fibrosis came to see us during that hospital stay. I have been able to call her whenever I need to talk about things or want to get some idea of what to expect. The most important healing for me, however, has come from having a pastor who willingly listens to my worst thoughts and fears.

In my work I see many people who are dealing with difficult and unexpected situations. What seems to matter most in their day-to-day living is not so much what has happened to them, but how they respond—the attitude they take toward what has happened. We can choose to focus on the good, considering ourselves blessed, or choose to focus on our problems, considering ourselves cursed. By God's grace, our family chooses to be blessed.

ELLEN L. AND ROB N. FILE

Ellen, a licensed local pastor, serves as Minister of Visitation and We Care Ministries at United Methodist Temple, in Beckley, West Virginia, where they live. Rob, an attorney, practices law in a local firm.

Reflection

1. When faced with something difficult and unexpected, how can we choose to be blessed?

2. How is a chronic situation different from an acute crisis? What does this suggest about how couples dealing with chronic situations need to take care of themselves? What kinds of help can others give?

> *Finally, be strong in the Lord and in the strength of his power. Put on the whole armor of God, so that you may be able to stand against the wiles of the devil.* EPHESIANS 6:10-11

Stitches in the Fabric of Our Love

Natalie and I were pleading our case before a judge in juvenile court. The police in another county of our state had arrested our youngest son on suspicion of something or other after he had dropped out of school and run away to follow a rock group. He had put us through worse times before, but this odyssey hadn't lasted long, thank God. Returned by our request to juvenile detention in our own county, he was not charged with anything this time, other than violation of the probation imposed as a result of previous juvenile offenses. Since he was almost eighteen now, this would be our last chance to intervene before the law would treat him as an adult. We begged for help: "Do something, Judge, anything. Just don't turn him loose to become more sick, more confused and angry. He already hates us, and we've done everything we know how to do by ourselves!"

Because our son was addicted to drugs, no one could have reached him at that point—not before he hit his "bottom." The Twelve-Step program and some of the many counselors we had seen with our son had stated this part of the equation correctly. The judge knew this, and so did we, but no one knew then just how far our son would have to fall to find his bottom. Without knowing this, we were unwilling to let him go, but the judge knew what she had to do. With a sigh of regret and a sad glance in our direction, she let him go without taking action. She let him fall; in doing so, she did the best thing she could have done for him. We know that now.

Although we had hoped for something else to happen, we were not really surprised by the judge's action. Now there was nothing left for us to do but to let him go ourselves. Even so, we tried again. We asked his probation officer if we could all meet together one last time. Our son came to the meeting elated, high on the prospect of freedom. We, on the other hand, felt devastated. He thought his ordeal was over. We knew it had only just begun.

We asked our son what he wanted to do: Would he like to come home with us now, or did he have something else in mind? When he said he didn't know, we helped him decide. We told him that if he wanted to live with us and go back to school or get a job, or whatever, he would have to live by our rules. There could be no drugs. Hearing that, he made up his mind. He told us that he loved us but, under the circumstances, he would be staying with friends until he could get enough money together to get a place of his own. With broken hearts, we understood him to be saying that he loved his drugs more than he loved us. Thunderstruck, I thought, *How could this have happened to us? What did we do that was so wrong?* Later, Natalie would audibly echo my thoughts.

After that day, seeking answers, understanding, and forgiveness, my wife and I separately shared our grief with friends. This helped some. We both also prayed individually, which helped even more. Attempting to put it all behind us, we threw ourselves into our individual work, which seemed to help the most. But we went up to our bedroom every night dreading our dreams and wondering silently to ourselves, *He's out there in the cold and the dark. Does he have a safe place to sleep tonight? Did he eat today? Is he well?*

Occasionally, our son stopped by to see us. Oh, how bittersweet those visits were! We let him come in, warm himself, bathe, and have a bite to eat. We tried not to give him money, but sometimes we did give him small amounts. Never, though, did we let him leave the house without food for later on. On other occasions, he sneaked into our house or garage to spend the night. Sometimes we heard him; sometimes we didn't. Sometimes he took something; sometimes he left something. But by morning he was always gone.

Months later, neither Natalie nor I had found peace. Neither of us understood what had happened, and neither of us felt forgiveness. Instead, we hit our own couple relationship bottom. It was as if the fabric of our love for each other was torn. Then God intervened, moving us to a different city in another state. That made it easier for us to stop enabling our son's behavior. Our individual sharing with others, our individual praying, the hours of individual distraction, and even our new surroundings, however, did nothing to mend our torn relationship.

Desperate and lonely, we decided to rededicate ourselves to what we had learned years before during a Marriage Encounter weekend. On that weekend we had learned an effective communication tool called "dialogue," which we started using again. Daily dialogues using the steps we learned during our weekend enable us to share on an emotional level. The structured approach helps us focus on what we feel, rather than on what we think. This has been easier for Natalie than for me, but over time I have learned to give myself over to my feelings more and more; and the change this makes in our relationship seems almost magical.

We had also learned during that weekend the difference between living together as a married couple (working and loving together) and living as a married-singles couple (working and loving separately). But then we became lazy, distracted, jaded, or something. Truthfully, I think we just let the challenges posed by our son's problems overwhelm us. Now we are stronger because of those challenges, but we had to work hard and work together to find our way back.

Fortunately, we knew what to do. We joined a couples support group in our new area, a Flame, as we call it in the United Methodist expression of Marriage Encounter. We also volunteered to serve as regional coordinators for Marriage Encounter in Eastern Missouri. Doing this meant that we had to give up some individual distractions, but it was worth it. Serving together in a ministry such as this keeps us focused and forces us to work at keeping our act together. This loving task placed us in the role of parents, in a sense, to other couples, and nothing reinforces learning like teaching and mentoring others.

Although we cannot assume all the blame for our son's problems, we have learned to accept our mistakes. Our biggest, I think, was our failure to be really together in our parenting. Natalie and I both tend to be competitive, especially with each other; our son became an expert at using this to his own advantage. When nothing else worked, he knew that he could always play one of us against the other to get his way.

Other couples who have had to face failures in parenting have helped us to forgive each other and ourselves. They've also helped us to focus on what we have done right and to stop punishing ourselves. One couple in particular always asked about our other sons, and smiled broadly when we spoke of their achievements. They knew something of failure themselves and shared this with us, but they also shared their successes. We learned a great deal from them. Now we give love and get it back as a couple again. Christ's love expressed through other couples has mended us; the stitches in the fabric of our love are by God's hand.

At the time of this writing, our son is working hard in recovery. Although he knows he is an addict and always will be, he also knows that he isn't powerless over his addiction. At least with God on his side, he isn't. And he knows that he isn't a bad person because of his addiction. Having completed a court-ordered rehabilitation program for adults, he is living clean and responsibly. Best of all, he has forgiven us and has embraced our Lord Jesus Christ as his own Savior.

KENT AND NATALIE GARRY

Kent, a government engineering services contractor and part-time Geographical Information Systems consultant, retired from active duty as a career Army officer in 1988 after twenty-two years of service. Natalie has worked in various nursing positions, including prenatal counseling, geriatric care, and public-health work. She serves as Parish Health Minister for Arlington United Methodist Church in St. Charles, Missouri, where they live. She is finishing her master's degree and postgraduate studies to become an advanced practice nurse. Kent and Natalie recommend *The Life Recovery Bible* as a resource for those facing problems with addiction.

Reflection

1. What does it mean to enable someone who has an addiction or is involved in other self-destructive behavior?

2. Have you ever had to take a "tough-love" position, as Kent and Natalie did with their son? Why is that sometimes necessary? How does it feel?

3. What does Kent and Natalie's experience tell you about communication? about parenting?

4. See "Toolbox: Communicating Feelings" (page 97) to explore the importance of feelings, techniques for expressing them effectively, and ways to demonstrate understanding and acceptance of someone else's feelings.

Contact information for Marriage Encounter is provided on page 120.

Caregiving Together

In 1985 my father, who had taken care of my invalid mother for the past twenty years, died on the operating table. Before our marriage, Brian and I had decided that we would become caregivers for our parents, if that should become necessary. Making that decision before we began our life together was one of the best gifts we could have given each other, because now we did not have to struggle in the heat of emotion over what we would do.

We moved into my mother's home and cared for her until her death a year and a half later. This was a good time of fellowship and growing, getting to know my mother in a special way. Brian and I, however, had to make many adjustments, as did our daughter, Lauren, who was five years old at the time. If we had not had such a strong relationship and good communication skills, some of those adjustments could have been disastrous.

Brian and I had full-time jobs as Salvation Army officers in Henderson, Kentucky, eight hours from my mother's home. My sister stayed with Mom for a week while Brian and I went home to pack and make the necessary arrangements. We requested a leave without appointment, with the option of returning to full-time service after completing our ministry with my mother. When Lauren and I returned to my mother's, Brian stayed in Henderson for another three weeks to wait for our replacements. The separation was hard on all of us.

By the time I arrived at my mother's house to stay, I was exhausted. Combining our two households was difficult, as I had to make it our home without leaving Mom out of any of the decisions regarding what we would use and what we would put away. Mother did not want to be alone, so I slept on a cot in her room. When Brian arrived, we took turns for several weeks sitting beside her bed. Needless to say, there was no private time for the two of us!

Brian began to look for work, but the city was economically depressed, and job openings were not readily available. One evening he went out to rent a movie, but he couldn't even do that because he was unemployed. He called me in tears and said he would be home later. I was upset about what Brian was going through and because I was unable to be with him. When he finally returned home, Mom was mad at him for staying out so late, I was hurt, and Brian felt devastated. Brian and I talked through the night and decided that something had to give if this arrangement was going to work. We decided that our marriage was even more important than taking care of Mom, and that we had to find time for ourselves and our relationship or find someone else to care for her. In the early hours of morning we talked, held each other, and moved into a new level of relationship beyond anything we had thought possible.

Brian finally found a part-time job as a cook at Pizza Hut and, after a while, another part-time position as a social worker at The Salvation Army in town. He left for work at eight in the morning and did not return until after midnight. These long hours left us little opportunity to be together, which created added stress for both of us. Eventually, The Salvation Army employed him full-time.

Things at home settled down somewhat, but Mom began expecting Brian to take my father's place in certain ways. She wanted him to serve as the handyman of the house, to tell her everything about his day at work, and even to whistle, which is something he hates to do. This didn't work at all. All day long she would complain to me about how selfish he was. When Brian came home from work at midnight, he would tell me how selfish and controlling she was. I spent all day mad at him and all night mad at her. Finally having had enough, I decided that this was their problem, not mine. That night I took Brian into her room, declared that I would no longer function as the go-between in their relationship, and told them to work it out themselves, taking whatever time they needed to do so. More than three hours later, Brian came out to tell me that she was ready to go to sleep. I still have no idea what they said to each other, but I had peace in my home once again. One of the hardest things we had to learn was that we were all individuals with different personalities. It took a lot of love for us all to treat each other as individuals and to work things out with one another.

Finances caused additional stress. We lived in Mom's house, but we still had our personal expenses. We got behind in paying our bills, which really bothered us. It was difficult to deal with Mom's fussiness about every penny we spent and her demands that we pay more of the household bills than we thought was fair. Again, Brian and I had to communicate lovingly and patiently with each other. Since it was Mom who was being unreasonable, I had to be the one to deal with her. She and I finally worked out a compromise about finances, and I again had peace in my home.

Maintaining any sort of normal sex life was a challenge. There were nights when she would call me to get up with her ten or twelve times. Not only were we constantly exhausted, but we were often interrupted during intimate moments. Brian is an exceptional man, full of love for me and, fortunately, patience. One particular night when she had interrupted us several times, I finally told her that I was really frustrated and that if she could give us thirty minutes, I would stay up with her all night. She did, we did, and I did. It was worth it! During this time in our marriage, we learned that intimacy is much more than sex. It includes just holding each other, kissing, and resting together at times. When you have limited time together, each moment becomes too precious to waste by fussing at each other.

Parenting offered us another challenge. We had always considered it the grandparents' privilege to spoil their grandchildren. Although we were still willing to allow some spoiling, we had to establish our authority and set boundaries for our daughter now that we were living with Grandma. It took a lot of communication for the three of us to clarify roles and responsibilities.

As Mom's kidneys failed, we knew that she was moving closer to death. She required more and more of my time, not always by her choice. I was often torn between being with her and being with my husband and child. I put a lot of pressure on myself and grew more demanding of Brian. Increasingly irritable, I lashed out at him with angry words, which caused him to step back from me because he didn't know how to help. We talked at length, trying to understand what was happening. Finally, I realized that I had to stop pressuring myself so much, and he understood how much I needed his support. Just being touched and held and told I was doing the right things eased my frustration. He also needed to be touched and held and appreciated.

When Mom passed away, Brian sat at one side of her bed and I at the other, each holding one of her hands. We prayed with her as she entered into the kingdom of heaven. When she took her last breath, Brian's presence gave me strength. During the next few weeks, as we made funeral arrangements and dealt with her will, he arranged for the sale of the house and did what he could to ease my way.

Throughout the year and a half of caring for my mother, we were grateful for any help we received from family and friends. We learned a lot about being caregivers and have since developed a class to teach others how to support people in that role. We encourage people to just show up when they can to sit with the person needing care, freeing the caregivers to spend time with each other and their children. I am grateful for my cousin who helped me after Mom's death to work through the feelings of loss and of not being needed in the same way anymore. In some ways, it was like losing a child.

Brian and I have been friends for years; we grew up together and have always been able to talk honestly and openly. We learned some effective communication techniques by trial and error and have led some enrichment groups out of our own experience. Every six months or so during the twenty-one years of our marriage, we have evaluated our relationship, affirming what is going well and facing what we could do better. This hasn't always been easy, but we have always learned and grown from doing so. Brian and I don't pretend to have a perfect marriage, but we do know it is a wonderful one.

Recently, we spent three glorious weeks camping, traveling alone together for more than ten thousand miles. We talked, laughed, cried some, and spent time in absolute silence. We discussed our relationship, the life we have shared so far, and even our retirement plans. And what could be better than making love under the beautiful sky of God's wonderful creation. We both agree that the opportunity to care for my mother, difficult though it sometimes seemed, gave us an opportunity to know each other in a different way, to deepen our relationship, and to take it to a whole new dimension.

LORETTA AND BRIAN GILLIAM

Brian and Loretta, with their daughter, Lauren, have moved to
Atlanta, Georgia, where they have returned to full-time assignments
with The Salvation Army.

Reflection

1. Why were Brian and Loretta able to come through this experience with a stronger and deeper relationship?

2. How do you intend to care for your parents if they need you to do so? What factors might influence your decision?

3. How do you hope to be cared for when you can no longer care for yourself? Use the process described in "Toolbox: Negotiating Solutions" (page 98) to discuss this or other issues.

Not Bound by Space and Time

Commentary

Increasing numbers of couples today find themselves having to live separately for a time, an experience once unique to military families. Large national and international corporations now dominate many employment fields, deploying their workers to distant locations without regard for the needs of other family members. Dual-career couples, in particular, face difficult choices when one is offered a promotion or transfer that narrows the other's options.

In the following stories, you will see how three couples have faced and coped with the challenge of nurturing their relationships and maintaining intimate connections, in spite of separation and limited time together. You will also see how frequent departures and homecomings can test a relationship and intensify underlying issues. We all probably would agree that married couples in general need to be able to communicate clearly, to negotiate in such a way that both parties get their needs met, and to recognize when outside help is needed. Living separately, as these stories illustrate, makes such skills essential.

Jonathan Livingston Seagull, in Richard Bach's little book by the same name, eased the sadness of a friend he was leaving behind by declaring that their friendship did not depend on space and time (page 87). Translating that ideal into an everyday reality requires creativity, as well as a commitment to stretch and grow.

Beloved, do not be surprised at the fiery ordeal that is taking place among you to test you, as though something strange were happening to you. But rejoice insofar as you are sharing Christ's sufferings, so that you may also be glad and shout for joy when his glory is revealed.　　　　　　　　　1 PETER 4:12-13

"Life Is Change; Growth Is Optional"

Although I had enjoyed serving a small rural church in Maine, I looked forward to a new appointment as an associate pastor in Rhode Island, with specific responsibilities in programming for children and families. Richard, however, needed to stay at his job in Maine for three more years in order to be vested in the state retirement system. After considerable discussion, we decided that I would take the appointment and that we would live separately for the necessary three years; but we would be together on weekends and as much other time as possible. Our younger daughter, Sarah, in her last year of junior high, came to Rhode Island with me. Our older daughter, Michelle, had just graduated from high school and was leaving for college. Richard's maintaining a home in Maine made it possible for Michelle, during college vacations, to continue to see friends she had made there.

Surprisingly, our living separately turned out to be harder on Sarah than on anyone else. Since I had a lot of evening meetings, she ended up alone much of the time. She went to friends' homes a lot, which made me feel guilty. We especially missed Richard when something unexpected happened, such as the night the car battery died when I was to drive her and a friend to a dance.

For Richard and me, however, the excitement of my new job and of this new stage in our relationship carried us through the first year. We learned a lot about ourselves and each other and worked at finding ways to keep our relationship alive. Someone had told us that when couples live apart, they just have to accept the fact that they will have big phone bills and not to worry about it. Talking on the phone was too much like business for Richard, which made it hard for us to get into personal dialogue. He was good about writing, and he often sent me cards and gifts during the week. Writing didn't work well for me, because my letters often didn't arrive until after he had been down to visit.

One interesting change was my attitude toward sex. During an earlier marriage enrichment experience, we had talked about my need to solidify our relationship and talk things out before moving into sexual sharing. Now, when we had been separated for most of the week, I found myself wanting to make love first thing when Richard arrived for the weekend. I guess it was a way of reestablishing our connection.

Richard found the three-hour drive exhausting, so after a few months he began to travel by bus and train. The trip took almost an hour longer, but he could read or sleep on the way, greatly relieving his stress and energy drain. Later, he was able to adjust his work schedule so that he left Rhode Island early Monday morning and worked from noon until eight at night, which gave us more time to do things together. It would have been a lot easier if I had not had to work on Sundays, or if I had not had a school-age child at home, so that I could have taken time off during the week to be in Maine. Sarah and I did visit Richard there during school vacations.

Near the end of the three years, Richard began to hint that he didn't really want to leave his job. I sensed that he wanted to renegotiate our agreement, but I just wanted him to move to Rhode Island as soon as possible. Although we had coped quite well with living separately, it was beginning to take its toll; and the tragic death of my twenty-year-old niece in an automobile accident threw me into depression. Another young niece had died earlier (also in an automobile accident), and my father had died when I was only twenty-two. I felt angry at God for allowing me to experience so much premature death.

I didn't want to burden Sarah with my grief, and my time with Richard was too short for me to process my feelings. Richard tried to be supportive, but he often slipped into giving advice, trying to fix it for me. I would get angry at him for not accepting my feelings. He tends to avoid conflict, out of his childhood experiences, so he withdrew from my anger. If we had not been living separately, I think we could have worked it through better; but I was stuck in my grief and frightened by his apparent willingness to continue living apart. I interpreted his uncertainty about leaving his job as pulling away from our marriage.

Later, I understood that he was really struggling with the issue of job security. He had a good salary and status at work, and he felt some lack of confidence about finding and moving into a new position. In addition, he had become comfortable living alone and keeping things neat and orderly; and he anticipated that life would be more hectic in Rhode Island, due to my erratic schedule and evening meetings. It was impossible for us to communicate effectively about all this during our brief visits. Fortunately, I was able to arrange for some counseling to deal with my grief issues and my fears in regard to our marriage.

Meanwhile, Richard's employer encouraged him to take a year's leave of absence to look for work in Rhode Island, assuring him that he could return to his job in Maine if nothing turned up. Richard sent out some resumes and, with the networking help of a friend in my church, soon located a good position. Once we were living together again, I regained confidence in his commitment to our marriage and in his desire for a supportive family relationship. Now we are discussing what we will do in retirement and thinking about what it might be like to have grandchildren. I am continuing to work with a therapist on my grief issues, and Richard and I have seen her together as well.

I think people marry because of their attraction to each other, but they then fall into rough spots and need impartial help working through them. I was not a minister when I married Richard, and he was quite surprised when I began to talk about going to seminary. He wasn't very supportive at first and basically left it up to me to do what I wanted. Within a year, however, he saw how I grew through my seminary experience and encouraged me to stick with it. We began to work with counselors, both separately and together, learning a lot about ourselves and how to relate to each other in a more nurturing way.

I know many couples have to live separately for periods of time, but we wouldn't recommend it, especially for those who have not been married a long time. Even knowing what our personal and relationship issues are, we slip back into old patterns under stress. Marriage enrichment experiences taught us to keep on talking, but participation in an ongoing support group would have helped even more. Life is a process or, as someone said, "Life is change; growth is optional." Our relationship has grown through several levels, and now we have moved into another, for which we are grateful.

SHARON AND RICHARD JONES

Sharon and Richard now live in Bristol, Rhode Island, where she serves as associate pastor in a United Methodist church and he works for Sodexho Marriott Services, Inc.

Reflection

1. If you and your spouse had to live separately for a time, what strategies might you use to keep your relationship alive and well?

2. Review "Toolbox: Two Ways to Improve a Marriage" (page 99), which outlines the differences between marriage enrichment and counseling. Do you consider seeking help a sign of strength or weakness? Why?

> *Like good stewards of the manifold grace of God, serve one another with whatever gift each of you has received.*
> I PETER 4:10

Frequent Flyers

We still smile warmly when we recall how we met in the bachelor officers' quarters laundry at Patrick Air Force Base near Cocoa Beach, Florida, where we each had just been newly assigned. We were both twenty-six years old and second lieutenants in the United States Air Force. Since I was not at all shy and found Ginny attractive, I invited her out to dinner. While expressing reservations about accepting an invitation from a fighter pilot, she did promise to think about it.

I hadn't been washing clothes all that often, but my laundry pattern changed right then and there. Soon we started dining out together at a variety of restaurants along the coastline. Over dinner we shared the new and exciting things happening in each of our lives. I was finally using the flying skills I had been certified for months earlier. Ginny was immersed in the fast pace of protocol and executive work for the base commander. She openly expressed doubts and shared concerns about her new job during our many evening walks along the beach. I remember trying to solve problems for her, but in hindsight realize that I did not share much about my own problems and doubts until much later in our relationship. We both had been living on our own for several years and had been in and out of relationships, none of them serious yet. We each had firmly established daily living habits and patterns, but we enjoyed being together and learning about each other.

After four months of duty in Florida, I was transferred to my permanent squadron at Shaw Air Force Base near Sumter, South Carolina. It was rough being apart, but this was only the first of many separations to come. We talked by phone frequently, and I got very familiar with I-95 down to Cocoa Beach and back. Sometimes Ginny would catch a military flight and visit for the weekend. After about six months of this, Ginny broached the topic of commitment when I was driving her to the airport one rainy day. I don't remember our exact words, but I know my hesitation hurt and frustrated Ginny. Many of my Air Force colleagues had told me about their marriage problems and their misgivings about having made quick decisions. On the other hand, I really respected Ginny and found her beautiful inside and out. My gut feeling was that it was now or never. Ginny made it clear that she was ready for marriage and that she had decided that I was her "prince for life."

We married six months later in a simple ceremony, in order to get official Air Force recognition and work toward getting assigned together. Then, six weeks later, we celebrated with a big wedding ceremony for family and friends. Although we came from different religious backgrounds—my family was Roman Catholic, and Ginny's Protestant—we were determined to center our marriage on a Christian foundation. Drafting an ecumenical service together with the military chaplain was a good first lesson in communication and negotiation.

We had to live apart for three months until Ginny could get assigned to Shaw Air Force Base. Then our marriage really started. Looking back on it, that first year in South Carolina was our toughest. Both being independent "type A's," with stubborn personalities, definite opinions, and a lot of pride, we frequently found ourselves in heated conflict. We were committed to making this relationship work, but we didn't have the tools to communicate effectively and negotiate our differences. One of the smartest moves we made was attending a weekend marriage enrichment retreat that was sponsored by the Shaw Air Force Base Chapel and the Association for Couples in Marriage Enrichment (A.C.M.E.). The communication techniques the leaders taught us were helpful, but we also had a lot to learn about creating intimacy, managing money, and dealing with anger, conflict, and the frequent separations required by our careers.

During that first year, Ginny's health suffered from the stresses of her move, a new and demanding job environment, her master's degree studies, and adjustments to our marriage. Because I come from a stoic and reserved family, I found it difficult to share feelings and communicate openly. This was hard for Ginny to accept, since she comes from a communicative Southern family. My schedule took me away from home, sometimes for a few days and sometimes for several months at a time, and the demands of flying added to my stress. Tension built as we approached a departure date and anticipated changing roles and responsibilities. We both did whatever needed doing at home, when we were there; but when one is gone for a time, the other has to take full control. My returns felt like a honeymoon at first, but we frequently found ourselves out of sync. For example, I would want to just stay home and relax, while Ginny was eager to get out to an auction or movie or just to do something together.

We tried hard to apply the techniques and skills we had learned from our A.C.M.E. weekend. We scheduled "cool-off" times and committed specific time for dialogue. We tried writing letters to each other, thereby more calmly explaining our respective points of view.

These strategies did help. Our love, commitment to growth, and desire for strengthened faith kept us progressing. Unfortunately, we often got so busy with our hectic, fast-paced, on-call jobs, along with caring for our new home and other commitments, that we would slip back into our old communication habits. There were no support groups nearby to help reinforce the skills we had learned in our weekend retreat.

Four years later we were reassigned to Holland, the country where I had been born and from which my family had immigrated when I was five years old. My fond childhood memories of that country, along with the chance to reconnect with my grandmother there, made that tour of duty a rich experience for us. Living in Europe offered us exciting opportunities for exploration and travel. The fast tempo of operations, including weekend and night duties, often overwhelmed us with job demands, but we found sweetness in growing together toward maturity in our marriage. Our mutual respect, trust, and love seasoned; but our communication and conflict-management skills did not progress much, especially with our continuing pattern of frequent separations. We would fight, yell at each other, and become defensive; then we would cool off and apologize, but without resolving whatever issue had triggered the argument.

Near the end of our overseas tour of duty, we resolved to reorder our priorities, let our military careers take second place, and find a way to stay together wherever we were assigned next. We both found challenging positions at the U.S. Air Force Academy in Colorado Springs, Colorado. Since we enjoy working with young people, this turned out to be a great place for us. Individually and together, we counseled young adult cadets about myriad issues, often academic but also related to family and personal concerns. We discovered real satisfaction in helping others, which, in turn, enriched us and our relationship. We were able to hone our marriage enrichment skills by leading premarital seminars, which were mandatory for couples planning to marry in the cadet chapel.

   When the time came for us to move on, after almost six years at the Academy, we couldn't find assignments that would keep us together. After many hours of discussion and with lots of soul-searching and prayer, we decided that Ginny would separate from active duty and enter the Air Force Reserves. It was a risk-laden decision, but it worked out well for her and for us as a couple. When I accepted an assignment in Germany, Ginny readily found a Reserve position, as well as an opportunity to teach college courses part-time. Because of the flexibility in her schedule, we could travel together much more than we had previously. We worked on nurturing our faith, both individually and as a couple, and we began to communicate better, which further enhanced our mutual love, respect, and trust. Dealing with anger and conflict, however, continued to be difficult.

   We stayed in Europe six and a half years this time; and as we neared the end of our tour, we decided that we needed to contribute more to the U.S. military community by sharing our marriage enrichment tools and experience. We knew this would help us keep growing in our own marriage as well. We attended a five-day training event of the Association for Couples in Marriage Enrichment back in the United States, and it was here that we decided to aggressively explore our still-unresolved difficulty with anger and conflict. We did not get angry often; but when we did, we hurt each other. Since we were unable to discuss such incidents rationally after the fact, we never got at the underlying issues.

   During open couple dialogue in our training session, with observation and feedback from the group, we realized that it was fear of my own temper that drove me to back off from conflict, because I was trying to regain my self-control and think through what was happening. By default, however, this usually ended the discussion. Ginny interpreted this behavior as an attempt to control her and manipulate the situation, although in fact it was my attempt to control myself. Upset by my withdrawal, Ginny would come on stronger, often saying things to get a reaction out of me. That, of course, just escalated my anger and fear. With a better understanding of these dynamics, we made a pact: I would post on the refrigerator a note stating that I needed thirty minutes to cool down, but that I would come back to the discussion after that time. We also agreed to practice daily sharing times, granting each other a full ten minutes of undivided, uninterrupted, and nonjudgmental attention to speak whatever was on our minds.

   Although we are less mechanical about it now, we still take regular time to really talk, listening to each other without interruption, judgment, or critical evaluation. The need for the cautionary note on the refrigerator has faded as our understanding of our dynamics has grown, along with our ability to accommodate each other's needs. During our recent move back to the United States, these improved skills certainly eased the way as we packed and shipped our belongings one more time, bought a new house, and established ourselves in a new situation. Sheer exhaustion and the frustrations of moving fueled some tense and angry moments, but we came through them without hurting each other.

As we begin our twentieth year together, we feel that God has truly blessed us. His grace has brought us through challenging times; and now, for the first time in our marriage, our jobs allow normal work hours and days, with few times of separation. Even when we must be apart, the departures and homecomings are less tense and conflicted, because we openly share feelings and talk about our concerns before, during, and after the separation. Although our Air Force careers are in their twilight, we have no regrets about making choices to strengthen our marriage rather than striving toward accelerated higher ranks and bigger pay-checks. Mentoring engaged couples through the Marriage Savers program in our church now gives us another opportunity to share what we have learned and to nurture our continuing growth.

MIKE AND GINNY DIETVORST

Mike and Ginny live in Montgomery, Alabama. While they were writing the first draft of this story, Ginny was diagnosed with breast cancer and now has successfully completed her course of daily radiation therapy. Secure in their knowledge of God's love and grace, they have been strengthened by prayer and the depth of their marriage relationship in facing what they consider their greatest challenge as a couple so far.

Reflection

1. What strategies does this story suggest for handling the stress of departures and homecomings, when couples must separate frequently and/or for considerable lengths of time?

2. How effectively do you deal with anger? See "Toolbox: Managing Anger" (page 100) to learn more about this powerful emotion and how to manage it for relationship growth.

Contact information for the Association for Couples in Marriage Enrichment and Marriage Savers is provided on pages 118 and 119.

Leap of Faith

have not seen my wife and children for almost three years now, since I came to Africa University to pursue my theological studies. I had hoped to bring them here to be with me, but have not had the money to do so. My plans to visit with them have been thwarted by war at home, as well as by the high cost of airfare back to Sierra Leone, which is more than a thousand miles away. Still, my faith and my prayers sustain me, and I have not given up my intent to trust God absolutely.

This was not always so for me. My life turned completely around when I was thirty-five years old. During a New Year's Eve vigil service in 1983, I resolved to serve the Lord totally; the following Sunday I gave my life fully to God to be used as an instrument of his will. Previously, I had convinced myself that my work as a music teacher was ministry enough, but then I accepted the call to be ordained and began my ministerial training during the next year.

In 1988 I graduated with honors from the Sierra Leone Theological Hall and Training Center, was ordained a deacon, and received an appointment to Trinity United Methodist Church in Moyamba for my final year of supervised practical pastoral work. In addition to my role as associate pastor, I soon found myself filling in as church organist, music teacher for the secondary school, school pianist, assistant school chaplain, and adult fellowship Bible-study leader.

I first noticed Mary, a teacher in the daycare program run by the United Methodist Women, sitting near the organ as I played for a service. We were introduced by her sister, the district superintendent's wife, who had been cooking meals for me, since I lived in the unmarried teachers' quarters and needed that support. Our courtship started in earnest when Mary took over from her sister the cooking of my meals. She also did my laundry and ironing, which was a great relief to me, since I had little time to spare from my studies and church work. We grew increasingly fond of each other and "adopted" each other's children: my five-year-old daughter, Doris, and her twenty-one-year-old son, Nathaniel. Our deepening faith motivated us to plan our future and life together with a common commitment to serve the Lord Jesus Christ.

Mary completed a training program to earn her certificate as an evangelist, after which she was hired by the Sierra Leone Annual Conference. I encouraged her always to pray over her salary and to budget it, first setting aside a tithe for the Lord. We became engaged in December 1990, and married the following April. At first we lived outside the school grounds, but later we moved into one of the apartments for married teachers inside the school's compound.

I longed to continue my studies in order to serve more effectively either as a pastor or teacher, and in 1991 I applied to the University of Sierra Leone. Courses there were suspended, however, because the rebel war had caused many of the lecturers to flee Sierra Leone to live in other countries. I had also applied to and been accepted at Africa University in Zimbabwe, but I did not have the necessary funds. The war, which had started just a month before our wedding, had caused rapid depreciation of our national currency, and we had spent much of our savings on the wedding.

Mary offered to use her own money to take care of our house, food, and children's school fees so that I could save my salary to pay for the examinations, airfare, and fees at Africa University. We considered other colleges, but, again, I had no way to pay. Africa University offered me financial aid, if I could only get to Zimbabwe. I wrote to the registrar there to request that my admission be deferred until 1993. Even still, it was difficult to raise money, and I had only about a third of the eight hundred U.S. dollars I needed.

One of the missionary teachers at the school in Moyamba suggested that I start a loan fund, requesting help from both the school and the church. She prayed with us and contributed twenty U.S. dollars herself every other month. Encouraged by this show of support, I continued to save my salary and plan for my journey to Zimbabwe. Another delay was caused by Africa University's change of schedule for its academic year. Finally, in August 1995, I enrolled as a freshman there.

I had hoped to participate in a work-study program for salary, in order to pay back the money we had borrowed for my airfare and to bring Mary and Doris to Zimbabwe to be with me. Unfortunately, work-study with salary was no longer available at Africa University. Also, Mary no longer had a job, because the rebel war had escalated and reached the Moyamba District in February. Fortunately, we had, by God's grace, escaped to Freetown, the capital city, where she now lives with my brother and his wife. It took all our savings to purchase my ticket; yet she still has to care for the children, her mother, my mother, and my younger brothers who are still in school. When my father died in November of 1996, she had to borrow money for the funeral expenses. She receives a ration from the world food program for war-ravaged and displaced citizens, and I send her what I can.

While I was mourning the passing of my father and praying for a way to get back to see my family, a volunteer-in-mission team member, who had come to Africa University to work on faculty housing construction for a week, went back to the United States and raised money for my roundtrip ticket home to Sierra Leone. I anticipated serving in an internship there, as well as reuniting with my family. Just about the time I was to go, however, the legitimate government was again overthrown by government soldiers, who had joined forces with the rebels. Economic sanctions and the trade embargo imposed on my country closed all its borders, airports, and seaports. Now, because the money had already been converted into Zimbabwean dollars in order to purchase my ticket and because Zimbabwean dollars have further depreciated in value, I no longer have enough money to go home when it is safe for me to do so.

Mary and I have been separated for almost three years now, but we still maintain our relationship through letters, telephone calls, and friends who convey messages for us. Our letters take about three months to arrive, since they have to travel through London first. Because telephone cards cost about twenty dollars in U.S. currency, we speak to each other by phone only once or twice a semester. My faith and prayers have been my most important source of strength. I start my day at five in the morning with a quiet time and a prayer for my family; and at each of our three meals, I think about them and pray that God will provide for them. At our fellowship meetings and worship services, I pray for my family, my sponsors, and my own needs. When I retire for the night and reflect on my day, I pray for them again.

When I finish my undergraduate course in divinity here at Africa University in May 1999, I want to begin the master of theology program. If we can get financial support for my wife and our daughter, Doris, to come join me in Zimbabwe, Mary might be able to attend one of the commercial training institutes here to learn dressmaking or catering, which would enable her to help support us. Or perhaps she could secure a position at a nearby boarding home. If they cannot join me here, I would be grateful for help in purchasing roundtrip tickets to Sierra Leone and back here once a year until I finish my studies.

A United Methodist missionary and lecturer at Africa University solicited funds from friends in the United States to assist married students in the School of Theology here. Although this amount of one hundred fifty U.S. dollars per year is small, it is at least an encouragement. I am grateful for this and all the other support Mary and I have received, but especially for prayers for my continued strength to pursue my studies and to triumph through this separation from my family and the troubles in my country.

ALFRED AND MARY WORLEY

At this writing, Alfred's family is still safe in Sierra Leone, although recently they were ordered out of their home by rebel soldiers, who searched and looted their house. Alfred, who recently completed a local church internship in Zimbabwe, still seeks to be reunited with his family and to continue his theological studies.

Reflection

1. Where does one get the courage and commitment to leave home and undertake such a difficult endeavor? For what goals would you be willing to make similar sacrifices?

2. How do the challenges described in this story change your perspective on your own life and blessings?

3. How do these hardships seem to have affected the Worleys' faith and prayer life?

4. How did you experience prayer in your family of origin? What spiritual disciplines do you practice in your current family? See "Toolbox: Nurturing Spiritual Growth" (page 101) to further explore this topic.

Love's Easter Song
Commentary

Dr. Patricia Love, speaking at the 1998 Smart Marriages/Happy Families conference, described our society as caught up in "post-romantic stress syndrome." Noting the popularity of movies such as *Titanic* and *Bridges of Madison County*, she commented that it is easy to love passionately for a few days and then to pine for the loved one the rest of your life. Sustaining passion in an ongoing relationship, amidst everyday demands and stresses, is much more difficult. Since much of the intense feeling produced by "falling in love" stems from newness and novelty, that intensity, unless intentionally nurtured, will fade in an ongoing relationship. As reality and familiarity set in, couples become aware of each other's imperfections and realize that marriage will not solve all their problems or completely heal the loneliness that is an essential part of being human. At this point, couples often struggle to change each other; some are quick to give up on the marriage. Blessed are those who work through this difficult stage to build an enduring relationship, based on deep mutual understanding and acceptance— both of self and of each other.

Couples who fail to anticipate these changes and lack the skills to nurture lasting love often react to fading passion and daily irritations by burying themselves in their work and other individual pursuits. Isolation and emotional distancing further erode their love, making them more vulnerable to extramarital attractions. In the following stories, couples bear witness to the pain of disillusionment and estrangement. Even more important, however, is their witness to the joy of healing and reconciliation. One contributor said, "We want others to know that no matter how hopeless your situation may seem, it is never too late to ask for God's help and to seek his answers for your life."

Let us therefore approach the throne of grace with boldness, so that we may receive mercy and find grace to help in time of need. HEBREWS 4:16

Repairing the Foundation

I noticed the first sign of a crack in the foundation of our marriage when we had been married four and a half years. Now I can see that the trouble really started about two and a half years earlier, when our son was born.

Frank and I met and fell in love during our college years. A mutual friend had kept trying to get us together, but it didn't happen until Frank just appeared on my doorstep one evening. My friend had kept saying we were perfect for each other, and we were. We fell in love almost immediately, even though he was four years younger than I. We had much in common, including our love of being outdoors, partying with friends, and just generally goofing around. My family and friends liked Frank just fine, even though they had expected I would marry a professional type, upwardly mobile and all that, like my father. Instead, I chose a free-spirited artist who wore shorts made from curtains, even in the dead of winter.

We had known each other for almost a year when I graduated from college and spontaneously decided to move to the Pacific Northwest. When I packed up my U-Haul and headed west, Frank came along for fun; but after three months, he returned to the East in time to register for the fall semester of school. I was crushed when he left, but promised myself I would stick it out for at least a year. I had a good job, but I missed Frank and my family so much that I cried every night. Around Thanksgiving, Frank finally called to say that he couldn't live without me and wanted to come back and be with me. I was elated. He finished his semester and worked long enough to save enough money to move. When he arrived on my doorstep the next spring, I knew it was forever this time.

We had incredible fun for the next four years. We traveled, camped, hiked, ate out a lot, went to concerts, made new friends, worked hard and spent our money on things we wanted. We were making a good life for ourselves, never dreaming that we would ever move back East. When Frank asked me to marry him, I said a big *yes*.

By this time, everyone in my family had accepted Frank for the person he was and appreciated that he loved me unconditionally. I could be completely myself with him. He loved me when I was bossy, grouchy, or even bratty. We never fought or disagreed. I was completely happy.

Two years after our wedding, Jack was born. I breezed through pregnancy and childbirth, not even needing shots or drugs for the delivery. Frank was supportive throughout the pregnancy and birth, pampering me the entire time. Jack was a beautiful, perfect, healthy child. My mother came to visit during the last few months of my pregnancy and stayed through the birth and for several weeks afterward. I was able to sleep all night while she got up in the wee hours to care for baby Jack. When she left, however, I think we both felt relieved to be alone again, although neither of us expressed that to the other. I didn't know it at the time, but Frank was beginning to feel a bit left out and neglected. He wasn't used to sharing me with anyone, especially someone so needy and precious as Jack.

I loved being a mom and made arrangements to stay home from work for nearly five months. As the time for my return to work drew closer, I panicked at the thought of leaving Jack in the care of a stranger in some germy daycare setting. After long hours of discussion, Frank and I decided to move back East, in order to raise our child in a safe, family environment. This seemed like a new adventure to us, and we both anticipated the change with excitement.

Back home, we found ourselves surrounded by family and friends. New time demands overwhelmed us, as we were not used to sharing each other with anyone else. Still reeling from becoming new parents nine months earlier, we began to drift farther and farther apart. During this time I started to attend church regularly, but sat alone on the pew. Frank said that since he didn't really believe in God, it would be hypocritical for him to go to church.

Although my family did not go to church while I was growing up, I attended Catholic schools and became interested enough in religion to participate in Mass and youth-group functions for several years. During my college years and after, I drifted away from church, filling my time with things that seemed more important. When I became pregnant, however, I started praying for the safety of our unborn child. I felt God's presence in my life and determined that when we settled into our new home, I would find a church, both for religious growth and for a true sense of community. Frank agreed to have Jack baptized, but he was not willing to attend church regularly. I felt truly at home in the church I joined, becoming a member of a women's circle and feeling myself grow spiritually. Frank resented the time and energy I was spending at church and felt that I was changing in a way he was not used to and had never expected.

Resentment sneaked into our relationship, along with various disappointments: We spent our savings and I had to return to work earlier than we had planned; Frank's dream of starting his own business failed; I spent too much time with my mother and sister; Frank started to drink too much; and the list could go on and on. We weren't ready to admit we had a problem; but I became increasingly unhappy, and Frank seemed to withdraw farther and farther from me. We both felt lonely.

That fall I made a new friend at work. He was a handsome, kind, smart, married man. We started having long discussions about religion, politics, current events, our families and childhood experiences, books, and music. The attention, time, and energy I spent conversing with and thinking about this man took away from my already-damaged relationship with my husband. By spring I realized that it had gone way too far. Although I had never touched him or discussed my feelings for him, I thought I was in love with him. One day I told him how I felt. He said he was flattered and that he valued me as a friend, but that he loved his wife and family and would remain faithful to them.

I mustered the courage, through lots of prayer, to tell Frank that I thought I was in love with another man. I knew that if there was to be any hope of saving our marriage, I had to start by being completely honest with him. He reacted with anger and hostility, which I had never experienced from him before. He said he needed time to think. It scared me to realize that I might be losing my dear husband. Fortunately, we found a counselor who could see us the next day. What a relief it was to be able to really talk about things honestly and to sense that we were moving in the right direction, instead of drifting farther apart. One of the first things the counselor said was that we had to stop blaming each other. She pointed out to Frank that my telling him the truth showed that I really loved him and wanted to make things better. She said that we obviously had a marriage worth saving, that she could see and feel the love and commitment we shared, and that she was sure we could make it through this treacherous time.

Over the course of the next few months, we read lots of books and did lots of "exercises." We made more time for each other and talked, talked, and talked. We had to learn to put others to the side and move our relationship to the top of our priority list. Through our counseling, we discovered many individual issues we had brought into our relationship that we needed to work on in order to make our marriage healthy again.

I had become so involved in parenting that I neglected Frank, putting him way down on my list of priorities. I had learned this pattern from my own mother, whose marriage had ended in divorce. Frank, having been raised in a traditional and emotionally neglectful household, did not know how to confront his feelings and express them in an honest way. Feeling abandoned by me, he simply withdrew into himself, a defense tactic from his childhood. This led to an endless cycle in which I, also feeling abandoned and lonely, put more time and energy into my relationships with our son, my family, and my friends. Our counselor pointed out to Frank that withdrawal had helped him survive an unhappy childhood; but in order for our relationship to grow and mature, he needed to learn to be honest with me.

We no longer attend counseling, but would not hesitate to return if we hit another bumpy patch in the road. We are on our way back, and we have the tools we need to maintain a healthy and honest relationship. We both realize that there is no quick fix, that a marriage is a work in progress. We will be fine-tuning our relationship from now until the end of our lives. Recently we celebrated our tenth anniversary, declaring our commitment to growing together forever. And with God's help, we will.

Perhaps the most dramatic sign of that is the fact that I no longer sit alone in the pew. Although Frank still struggles with faith issues, he comes to church with me now, having realized how important it is to me and that it is a way for us to continue to grow together.

ANONYMOUS

Reflection

1. Scott Stanley, in *The Heart of Commitment*, compares marriage to financial capital, which requires regular, steady investment in order to thrive (pages 117–22). Recall the story Jesus told about the faithful and unfaithful servants in Matthew 25:14-30. Make a list of things you can do to invest in your marriage: specific acts of kindness and appreciation that show your spouse that he or she is high on your priority list. Plan to carry out at least one of these every day.

2. Another way to invest in your marriage is to do things together. Make a list of activities you both enjoy, of individual interests you could share with each other, and of new things you could learn together. With your spouse, agree on at least one of these and put it on your calendar for the near future.

> *But God, who is rich in mercy, out of the great love with which he loved us even when we were dead through our trespasses, made us alive together with Christ—by grace you have been saved.*
>
> EPHESIANS 2:4-5

Restoring Our Love

Diane and I met as pen pals while I was in the Navy and she was in college. She wrote long, wonderful, caring letters at a time when I was especially lonely, and I shared with her my deepest feelings and dreams. When we finally met, about a year later, she was even more beautiful than I had dreamed. After that, our letters became more intense and personal. One day, when my ship's radio reported a riot and shootings at Kent State, where she was attending classes, I worried for several days over whether she had been wounded, arrested, or worse. When I finally received a letter telling me that she was all right, I knew how important she had become to me. From then on we spent as much time together as we could, until I finally flew to Ohio for our wedding. Then I reluctantly returned to overseas duty for three more months.

Even though we began our marriage living in a mobile home at a Naval Air Station, Diane and I remember this as a happy time. She taught school, and we spent our free time together hiking, leading Scout troops, cuddling, making love, and dreaming of our future. We thought we had our own little slice of heaven. Every time I went to sea, I was overwhelmed by such loneliness and sadness that I resolved to leave the Navy as soon as I could. I wanted to spend all of my time with Diane.

I thought the romance in our marriage would continue and grow once I no longer had to go to sea for months at a time. I felt insecure financially, however, and started working part-time while taking classes at the university. Diane's new teaching job required her to spend twelve to fourteen hours a day doing schoolwork. Between her schedule and mine, we found little time together for talking, sharing, or intimacy. Diane's parents tended to interfere with our lives, generously purchasing property where we could keep our mobile home, but then, without even consulting us, arranging with our contractor to change our plans for a small garage to a two-story building with space for them to stay when they came to visit us. I often felt angry at Diane because of her parents' meddling, but I couldn't figure out how to solve this problem.

I had what I thought were pretty normal expectations when Diane and I married. Although in some ways my mother was a typical housewife, my parents shared many tasks and responsibilities. I assumed Diane and I would do the same. Somewhere in my twelve years of strict parochial-school education I got the idea that sex was a daily expectation in marriage, and that neither spouse was permitted to deny the other's requests for intimacy and sex. Diane, on the other hand, grew up in an undemonstrative family; her parents worked hard and seldom seemed to have fun or show affection for each other.

After we married, I gradually became more and more preoccupied with my hobbies and interests, which included stamp collecting and photography. I was disappointed in our sex life, which just didn't live up to my expectations, and I often felt frustrated and angry. Diane loved to shop and never seemed satisfied with what she had, even when her closets were bulging. She also spent hours working out, running, and participating in various fitness programs. When our first child was born, we started attending church because that seemed to be the right thing to do; but we never spoke of God or religion to each other. Our children knew nothing of spiritual life at home, except for a few religious story-books we read to them.

As the years continued, Diane seemed less and less interested in sex or any kind of intimate relationship with me. We argued a lot, which upset me, and I would usually either walk away or agree to do something I didn't really want to do. Since she had to get up earlier than I did to go to work, I could avoid being with her by staying up later at night to work on something or to watch television. After we started going to church, I ran for parish council and joined the Knights of Columbus. Other volunteer activities added to my excuses for getting out of the house. We even took some separate vacations, since we taught in different school systems that had different spring breaks.

Diane worked late at her school grading papers and preparing lessons, often not even coming home for dinner. She developed close friendships with her colleagues and enjoyed spending time with them. Our actions communicated that we did not consider each other or our marriage important and that we should not expect much from each other. Later we would understand this as a married-singles lifestyle, which means that we pursued individual goals at the expense of our marriage. At the time, however, I justified my distancing behavior by telling myself that at least we were still married, unlike many of our divorced friends and family.

I became increasingly annoyed by some of Diane's habits, such as spending what seemed like hours on the phone. Our sex life bottomed out, and we finally sought marriage counseling, after which things were better for a while. When our daughter was born, we moved into a large older home in town. I was delighted with the space, the neighborhood, and with not having so much grass to mow; but my hopes for a loving marriage faded as my new teaching job and the birth of our son resulted in even less quality time for Diane and me. As we drifted back to our old ways of blaming and fighting, I longed for the warm, intimate sharing we had experienced early in our relationship. I blamed Diane for our problems and intentionally withheld affection from her and the children.

Diane stayed home for a while after our son was born, although she loved teaching and missed her colleagues and students terribly. She loved being with her babies, but seemed overwhelmed by parenting and household responsibilities. The children were sick a lot, and the house was such a mess sometimes that she parked the vacuum cleaner beside the front door so that guests would think she was about to clean. I understand now that she resented my going off to the professional world while she stayed home, and that she hated hearing about my work because she was jealous of my professional life. Often I would promise to help around the house and then not follow through. Sex was sporadic, and we never really talked anymore. The close understanding and special feelings we had once shared were buried under hostility, loneliness, and sadness.

I know now how fruitless it is for married couples to carry their hurts around, adding to them regularly, storing them up so that they can be called to the surface at a moment's notice. I would pretend I was listening to Diane when she spoke, but instead I was paying attention to something else, often the television or the newspaper. I would answer her in a compliant manner just to avoid conflict. I never promised to do anything anymore, saying only that I would "try," which gave me a ready-made excuse when I didn't get around to it. Although she told me many times that all she needed from me when she was upset was a hug, I withheld that simple comfort, punishing her for not meeting my needs. When it appeared that we didn't have time together for an evening out or for intimacy and sex, I criticized her for the amount of time she spent on her students, her work, her exercise, and her friends. Nursing my hurt over how unimportant I seemed to be to her, I avoided her as much as I could, and that hurt became more important to me than her needs or our relationship.

Diane began to suffer from migraine headaches, which came on weekly, lasted up to three days, and caused even more deterioration in our relationship. Although I would take over all the family responsibilities, I failed to support her emotionally. When the children both started school, Diane was desperate to return to teaching; but with her master's degree and years of experience, she had to accept a position that required an hour's commute each way. With the stress of teaching emotionally disturbed adolescents, her migraine headaches continued almost every week. She arrived home exhausted and angry, often going straight to bed. Her depression deepened, and she barely slept or ate.

Diane seemed to dedicate all her time and energy to her school and students, leaving none for me and little for our children. Frustrated and angry, I retaliated by withdrawing even farther. Occasionally, I tried to listen to her concerns, but responded by giving answers I thought she needed. She didn't seem to want the suggestions or solutions I offered, which confused me: *Why would she try to talk to me if she didn't want my help?* We argued more and more often, each of us trying to win the arguments. I shut Diane out of my life, assuming that she wanted us to lead separate lives and each deal with our own problems. As I took over more and more of the household and parenting responsibilities, I often found myself saying mean things to her. If she wouldn't find time for us, and especially for my sexual needs, then I wouldn't find time for hugging her or showing any kind of affection. Diane became even more angry, depressed, and defensive.

One day when she was especially upset, I tried to calm her and convinced her to sit on the couch with her head in my lap. Broken and desperate, she confessed to me that one of her colleagues at work had been giving her the understanding and support she was not getting at home. This friendship had suddenly progressed into sexual intimacy, which she did not want but was unable to resist because she feared losing his support. This man threatened to expose her and ruin her career if she refused to continue a sexual relationship with him. She intended for it never to happen again, but felt guilty and frightened, in addition to missing the emotional support he had provided.

Emotionally paralyzed and inflamed by anger, I left Diane in tears and went up the street for a long walk. I considered what would happen to our children if we got a divorce. Remembering Diane's severe depression, I began to fear that she might try to commit suicide. Realizing that I still had feelings for her and wanted her back and happy again, I went home. We talked and cried for hours, but didn't solve anything.

Diane started counseling; but when she had a bad experience with a judgmental psychologist, she stopped seeing him. Late one night I took her to see our pastor, the only person she seemed to trust. She spoke of feeling worthless, embarrassed, and terrified. I discovered that she kept a razor and towels stowed in her car, in preparation for ending her life. I was terrified, certain that I couldn't survive if she killed herself.

A friend at church told us about Retrouvaille, and as a last-ditch effort, we decided to go for a weekend. Knowing nothing about the program, I started the weekend with many doubts. We practiced the dialoguing technique the presenters taught us, although at first I kept slipping into trying to fix things. It took me a while to realize that problems that had developed over years couldn't be solved in one night or one weekend. Finally, I began to understand Diane's feelings and my role in the break-down of our marriage. I learned how my failure to listen or to pay attention to her needs had caused her to give up on me. Promising to do things, making excuses, and then accusing her of nagging when I failed to follow through was a form of emotional abuse. It made me sad to realize my part in our problems, but I eventually realized that our marriage would never improve unless I understood and accepted my share of responsibility. It was a relief, however, to know that there was a chance for us to rebuild our relationship.

My accepting some of the responsibility for all that had gone wrong between us seemed to lift a burden from Diane's heart. She needed my love and forgiveness, but had been reluctant to ask for it, accept it, or believe in it. I needed her forgiveness for all the years during which I had displayed indifference and ignored her emotional needs. We held each other and cried, feeling a peace and closeness that we hadn't shared in many years. The decision to look for love in each other, to stay married, and to try to heal the pain we have caused each other is the glue that has held us together through our daily struggles.

ANONYMOUS

Reflection

1. What expectations did (or do) you bring to marriage? How realistic are they?

2. The post-marital experience of "falling out of love" is a normal phase in the shift from infatuation to genuine love. Unfortunately, this couple got caught in a destructive pattern of distancing and withholding, each blaming the other for failing to provide validation and support. It took a crisis and the Retrouvaille weekend to break this cycle. What can we learn about building a healthy relationship from this couple's story?

Contact information for Retrouvaille is provided on page 120.

*If it had not been the L*ORD *who was on our side…, then the flood would have swept us away, the torrent would have gone over us.*   P*SALM* 124:1*a*, 4

To Heal the Hurt

When Ruth went back to work after the birth of our first child, I was, on the surface, happy to give up my career to take care of our daughter. Underneath, however, I felt inadequate as a man. I couldn't admit it, but a part of me believed that I was supposed to be the breadwinner and take care of everything for my family. Even when I began to work again in the evenings, Ruth and I bickered constantly about money, housework, and in-laws; but I couldn't bring myself to admit to her how hard I was struggling.

Another woman seemed to offer a cure for my shaky self-esteem and unacknowledged frustrations. I knew that the physical part of the affair was wrong, but I deluded myself about the danger of my emotional involvement, which continued for a much longer time. This delusion enabled me to justify giving someone else the care, comforting, and nurturing that belonged to my wife and child. I know now that the minute you find yourself needing to lie about your relationship with someone of the opposite sex, you are involved in something that will damage your marriage and hurt those you love most.

Ruth sensed something was wrong, but had no real evidence until the other woman's mother called her one evening, a couple months after it had ended, to tell her about the affair. When I came home that night, I finally got what I deserved. Frightened, hurt, and hysterical, Ruth screamed and cried, threw things, and hit me. I denied that I had been unfaithful. When she told me to leave, it was the darkest night of my life. The realization of what I had done was suddenly placed squarely on my shoulders, and it was too heavy for me to carry. Believing that everyone would be better off without me, I came very, very close to killing myself.

God, however, had other plans for me. As morning came, while I was focusing on how badly I hurt, God made me realize that I had brought it on myself, while Ruth and our child, who had witnessed our bitter fighting, had no choice in their pain. In panic and desperation, realizing there was no way I could fix what I had done, I called Mark, a friend from work who had recently encouraged us to attend his church. Little did I know how important that phone call would be.

After calling Ruth to let her know he was praying for her, Mark spent the day with me, sharing the story of a crisis in his own marriage. Mark assured me that the healing of their marriage was not anything they had done, but was something God had done through them. For the first time, I felt hope that Ruth and I might have a chance to save our marriage. Mark spelled out the hurt that I had caused Ruth and how humble and hard the road was going to be if I wanted her back. There was never any question about that. I realized how much I truly love Ruth, and I was dumbstruck at how totally stupid I had been.

Mark called a couple in his church who do marriage counseling, and they offered to drop everything and see us that evening, if Ruth would agree. When I finally admitted my guilt to her, she was already changing bank accounts and planning her escape from the ruins of our marriage. I thought she had been angry before, but now the flood gates of her anger opened wide. Not only the affair but also the fact that I had lied about it had completely destroyed her trust.

Mark prayed with and for her, persisting until he finally convinced her to meet me at the counselor's home. In spite of the tension between us, I felt real peace about being there; but Ruth visibly shook with humiliation and anger. From the beginning, the counselors made it clear that they had no interest in working with us if we were just going to get a divorce. My response to that was easy, but Ruth felt put in a tough spot. She said she could not understand how she could ever trust me or feel the same way about me again, which was a real slap of reality for me.

The counselors insisted that we start attending church regularly and that I move back home that night. Ruth objected, but they insisted that they were committed to putting relationships back together and that we had to work together on this. I was happy when Ruth gave in, but I had no idea how hard it was going to be. Although constantly aware of the hurt and disappointment in Ruth's eyes, I found myself totally helpless to comfort her. I had to face the fact that I had become what I never wanted to be: an unfaithful, untrustworthy liar.

But God is good! Over time, the counselors helped us work through the roots of our problems and find better ways to communicate. They pulled the words and feelings out from behind our hurt, teaching us methods such as writing down our feelings and restating the other person's thought before responding. At first the feelings we communicated were raw and painful, and I was confronted with the reality of the hurt I had caused.

After several months filled with a great deal of mistrust and anger, we slowly began to make little improvements and finally made it to a different place in our marriage. One night, during the drive home from a session with the counselors, Ruth felt really touched by a song on the Christian music radio station. She admitted to me that night that she understood how she had contributed to our rocky marriage, that she could see how sorry I was for having hurt her so, and that she was ready to forgive me and start over. For the first time in ages, we talked without anger and mistrust, experiencing a much-needed cleansing. We were intimate that night, and things felt right again.

We still had difficult times after that, but we have learned a lot and now have a marriage based on honesty and openness—nothing like what it was before. We have had to work harder than we have ever worked on anything before, but we are proud of what we have accomplished—what God has done through us. We have been supported and encouraged throughout by Mark and his wife and several other couples in our church who have been through similar crises themselves. We are so grateful to them and to the counselors, whose difficult ground rules forced us to deal with each other and work things out when it would have been easier to split. God placed in our lives people who loved us and carried us through this crisis, not just because we are friends, but because that is how God wants us to live.

We now have a second daughter—truly a gift from God. I pray that I can be the kind of husband and father our daughters can be proud of and that someday each will say that she wants to spend the rest of her life with a man who loves her the way her dad loves her mom. I will spend the rest of my life trying to heal the hurt I have caused, and I am grateful for the opportunity to do so.

ANONYMOUS

Reflection

1. What does this story tell us about the pain infidelity causes?

2. What does it take to heal a marriage after infidelity has occurred?

3. Read "Toolbox: Nurturing and Protecting Your Love" (page 102). What can couples do to protect their relationship from the seduction of extra-marital attractions? to heal their marriage if infidelity has occurred?

Behind Our Masks

Karl and I, married for eighteen years now, have four children (two teenagers and two preteens). We live in a plain little house in the country and go to church every Sunday. Everyone probably thinks of us as the perfect family, but they don't know what goes on behind our doors. Karl and I wear our masks well.

When I turned thirty several years ago, I began to look at myself and didn't like what I saw: a quiet, hesitant woman with little self-esteem. While I had spent the last ten years having babies—stuck at home and changing diapers—Karl was usually out somewhere. He is a hard worker and supports us well, but he really likes participating in sports tournaments. Sometimes it seemed as if once I said "I do," he knew that he had me and didn't have to relate to me anymore. Karl and I were lonely even when together because we didn't know how to share true intimacy.

While Karl is outgoing, I am very introspective. I tend to keep things inside and find it hard to communicate my real feelings. Karl often came home late, so he missed supper. I was eager to talk to him about my day, but he didn't seem to have much interest in talking. He approached me for sex, but that seemed to be all I was good for. Often lonely, I began going out with girlfriends to sit around and talk and have a few drinks. Looking back, I feel guilty about how much time my children spent with baby sitters; but going out with my girlfriends was important to me then. I found that drinking opened me up and helped me stop thinking negative thoughts about myself. These outings helped me avoid the feelings of loneliness and emptiness bottled up inside me.

About this time, I received a phone call from a man I didn't know, who claimed that he had seen me out with my friends and found me attractive. At first I thought it was just a prank, so I hung up on him. He called again;

this time he was more flirtatious and seductive, saying how much he wanted to have sex with me. At first I thought he was crazy, but it was also exciting. For more than a year he continued to call, doing most of the talking while I listened quietly. Gradually I convinced myself that I could do what he was suggesting. Sometimes, when he hadn't called for a while, I called him. My loneliness and low opinion of myself made me vulnerable to his seductive ways, which made me feel good again—but not for long. He stated clearly that he was interested in sex only, not a relationship. He admitted to being into "swinging" and pornography. I knew I wasn't his first target, and probably not his last.

When we finally met, I felt nervous and uncomfortable. He touched me gently and spoke seductively, urging me to relax and promising that he would leave if I asked him to. I was afraid to say anything, afraid he would leave, afraid of being lonely again. At least he noticed me! Becoming numb to the probable consequences, I rationalized that everyone else was experimenting sexually. I thought I could have the excitement of this affair without it affecting my family.

Karl continued to busy himself with work and sports, and I escaped into the fantasy of this affair. Being with this other man was addictive. It was like getting a fix—feeling good for a while, but afterward feeling empty again. It wasn't that we had sex that many times; but each time we did, something inside me died. Then I would come back to him again, wanting to enjoy his acceptance and interest in me. Karl and I and our children still went to church as a family, but we were spiritually blinded. Church gave us an opportunity to socialize, but our eyes were closed to the Word of God.

As I got deeper into this mess, confusion tore at me and I became more and more dysfunctional. My guilt and fear built up, and I became more impatient with my children, yelling at them and neglecting their needs. Karl and I became more and more distant. I tried to tell him how unhappy I was with the way our life was going, but he didn't see anything wrong. I continued to go to the other man's place. Although he was skillful at manipulating me, I thought I controlled him with my appearance and the way I dressed. He enjoyed pornography, and I know now that he had a sexual addiction. Karl and I began to watch pornography, too. We had no idea it could be so addictive and destructive to our lives. After a while, pornography creates dissatisfaction with normal sex and a hunger for something new. The more distant I became from God and Karl, the more I started to crumble and feel that my life was out of control. Lying to Karl made me feel personally bankrupt.

Finally, after much struggle and discussion, Karl and I decided to participate in a Marriage Encounter weekend. I was at my wits' end, getting deeper and deeper in trouble, but wanting desperately to get out. Participating in the weekend meant that Karl had to give up a hockey tournament, but he could see it was important to me. His willingness to do that showed how much he loves me, in spite of the lack of intimacy in our relationship. That weekend made me look clearly at myself, our relationship to each other, and our relationship to God. In distress, I acted coldly toward Karl, even telling him Saturday night that I didn't really love him. We had heard the presenter couple say, however, that love is a decision, not a feeling. We asked them for some private time for extra help.

Mark and Connie, the presenter couple, are not trained counselors, just ordinary people who prayed with us and encouraged us to communicate honestly with each other. They gave us the following Bible verse to use for daily focus: "For surely I know the plans I have for you, says the LORD, plans for your welfare and not for harm, to give you a future with hope" (Jeremiah 29:11). It was an emotional weekend, as our eyes were opened to each other and to God. During the next week I finally told Karl about my affair. Mark and Connie, in whom we confided, supported us through this time, calling daily for a while and then at least once a month to encourage us as we found our way back to each other. We are so grateful to them for believing in us and supporting us through these difficult times.

Karl was heartbroken when I told him, and we cried and argued a lot at first. He asked a lot of questions, wanting to know all the details, but I didn't really want to talk about it. At first, when Karl seemed weak and overwhelmed, I felt strong. But the stronger he became, accepting what had happened and willing to do whatever it would take to rebuild our marriage, the weaker I became. It took me nine months to reach the point where I could promise Karl that I would stay and try to make our marriage work. At first I didn't believe him when he said he would change, but he was determined. He bent over backward and forward to please me and win back my love. We went to marriage counseling for about two years. Now we do devotions and pray together, and by God's grace we have made it back together.

It is now four years since that Marriage Encounter weekend. During that time I have struggled with anger, resentment, and self-doubt. I isolated myself from the world for a while because I was afraid of making a mistake like that again. Deep in depression, I lost my joy in life and found it difficult to cope with daily stresses. I am gradually recovering now, thanks to medication prescribed by my doctor and the guidance of a counselor, who is helping me see who I am and why I do the things I do. With the encouragement of our minister, who has been supportive, Karl and I joined a Twelve-Step support group at our church, where we can share what happened to us without fear of being judged. This was frightening to me at first, as I could not imagine telling my story to anyone; but I finally became desperate enough to try it. I still feel uncomfortable when new people come into the group. We use a Bible-based resource book, *The Twelve Steps for Christians*, and I am learning to take one day at a time searching for the love of God, accepting my mistakes in the past, and gaining courage to change the things I can in the present. When I have a bad day, for example, I make sure Karl and the children understand that it is not their fault, while at the same time telling them what I need.

I feel sad for the years when I could not communicate to Karl my loneliness and lack of self-esteem. I feel sad when I look back on my life and face how I have lived. The consequences don't disappear, but by grace I am healing and we are building a new life. Karl and I now have a special relationship. I have found in him the friend I longed for, and we experience God's presence in our everyday lives.

ANONYMOUS

This couple recommends three books that have been helpful to them: *Love Life for Every Married Couple: How to Fall in Love, Stay in Love, Rekindle Your Love,* by Ed Wheat and Gloria Okes Perkins; *Rekindled,* by Pat and Jill Williams, with Jerry Jenkins; and *An Affair of the Mind: One Woman's Courageous Battle to Salvage Her Family From the Devastation of Pornography,* by Laurie Hall.

Reflection

1. Intimacy in marriage grows as each partner develops more honest self-awareness and willingness to share openly with the other. Intimacy grows as couples develop a high degree of caring and trust and learn to be emotionally present to each other. Healthy intimacy strikes a balance between autonomy and interdependence and ebbs and flows, growing and changing through the seasons of marriage (*The Intimate Marriage,* by Howard and Charlotte Clinebell, pages 24–28). When have you felt most intimately connected to another person?

2. The Clinebells list and describe various kinds of intimacy: sexual, emotional, intellectual, aesthetic (sharing experiences of beauty), creative, recreational, work, crisis, conflict (dealing with differences), commitment, communication, and spiritual (pages 28–39). Which of these do you consider to be strengths in your marriage? Which would you like to develop more fully?

Choosing to Love and Forgive

We married in the mid-70's, with hopes and dreams like those of many Christian couples. Having found each other in a Bible study group, we attempted to make Christ the center of our lives and marriage. Unknowingly, however, we brought considerable baggage into our marriage and experienced many conflicts. Because of our faith, however, we thought our problems would magically disappear. Ill health and a demanding family business put additional strain on our relationship. We often argued and fought until one of us left our small apartment to sulk or cool off.

Two years after our wedding, our first child was born. I was away at work much of the time, and we lived a considerable distance from our parents. Julie, alone with our new baby for long periods of time, felt isolated and depressed. We had searched unsuccessfully for the perfect church. When a new one started up in a nearby town, we thought it was the answer to our prayers. The pastor, his wife, and their two delightful children seemed friendly and compatible, as did the other church members we met. The pastor was also a licensed marriage counselor, which probably helped the church to grow. Soon we were pouring concrete and hammering nails for a new and larger building.

Being a Christian was my most important goal, as well as being a good husband, but I was uncertain how to achieve either. I believed that if I earned a decent living for my family and served God through the church, everything else would magically take care of itself. This new church seemed to provide God's direction for my life. Although my job frequently took me out of town, I was eager to help at the church whenever I was home. We both became more and more involved: teaching church school, playing on the church softball league, helping with youth activities, and serving coffee before church services. When our second child was born, the church family jumped right in to help.

We were still having marital problems, but I couldn't figure out why. After a while, we started counseling with the pastor, which seemed to help at first; but then we started having the same old ups and downs, with the downs getting lower and lower. I was determined to make our marriage work, but I wasn't sure how to demonstrate my love for Julie in a convincing way. Julie, lonely because I was so busy at work and at church, suffered from depression and continued to counsel with the pastor. He convinced her that I was a big part of her problems and that he could make her happier. Going against everything she knew to be right, Julie allowed herself to be caught up in this relationship. The pastor seemed really interested in her as a person, and she thought she was finding the fulfillment and happiness she had been seeking.

Numbed by guilt and remorse, Julie became even more involved in church activities and in "counseling" sessions with the pastor through the next eleven years. Completely unaware of what was happening, I often stayed home with the children, rationalizing that it was for the kingdom of God and that I should be willing to share my wife with the church. Finally one day, as Julie describes it, she looked into the mirror and thought about what she had gotten herself into. The cold waters of reality washed over her as she realized that what she had been offered was only an illusion and that she had walked away from what was truly worthwhile. She struggled to find a way out of this mess without destroying our family.

I was puzzled when Julie begged to move to another town, as there seemed to be no logical reason for such a change. Then church attendance started to drop, and rumors spread around town about the pastor having affairs. I persuaded others on the church board that since these rumors could not be substantiated, they did not provide grounds for firing him. When the pastor's wife filed for divorce and the board voted to close the church, I was devastated to see our hard work, friendships, and the church's ministries going down the drain.

The pastor stayed in the area and continued his counseling practice. Julie, struggling under a load of guilt, shame, and depression, finally confided in two other women who were her good friends in the church. To her horror, they confessed that they, too, had been seduced by the pastor. They decided that they could liberate themselves only by confronting him together. Julie asked me to follow them to the church office, but did not explain why. After the confrontation, she came out and got into my truck, knowing in her heart that she had to be honest and risk everything if she were truly to make a clean break.

While waiting in the truck, I had been considering the rumors about the pastor and his alleged affairs and had begun to worry that they might be true. As Julie slipped into the truck, I turned to her with a fearful heart and asked if she was one of the rumors. Tearfully, she nodded yes. The pain of the church's closing was insignificant to what I felt at that moment. My worst nightmare had just come true. I felt tortured and numb, as if my life were being drained from me. Julie was the only woman I had ever loved, and I couldn't understand how she could betray our marriage vows.

Then a strange strength surfaced from deep within my heart, and forgiveness and compassion began to overpower my first reactions of hurt and anger. I believe that was the power of God at work. After what seemed like an eternity, I put my arm around Julie and told her I forgave her and that I believed we could make it through this tragedy together if she was willing. For Julie, this moment felt like a rebirth. Even though she knew there were many issues to work through, she felt new hope. With God's help we would work through this. The weeks and months that followed were filled with tears, remorse, and grieving. The rebuilding of our relationship was extremely painful, but the Holy Spirit and our faith in a loving, forgiving God made it possible.

Realizing that she needed real help for her depression and low self-esteem, Julie sought out a female Christian psychiatrist, who provided counseling and prescribed medication for more than a year. When I suggested participating in a Marriage Encounter weekend, the psychiatrist encouraged us to go, convinced that we had made enough progress in dealing with our underlying issues to benefit from the experience. The weekend was wonderful! We were able to share feelings and hopes in a way that we had not believed was possible. We finally achieved the kind of intimacy Julie was so desperately seeking when she "took the poison apple." I underwent a profound change as I learned to open up my inner self and communicate with Julie on an emotional level that seemed terrifying at first. Having grown up with an alcoholic mother and an abusive father, I had no role models for a loving relationship. I had kept my emotions buried deep and had resisted Julie's attempts at intimate communication.

Learning to really love Julie involved risking and sharing as we opened ourselves to each other's hopes and dreams, hurts and fears. It meant learning to consider her needs, even when it is inconvenient or when I don't understand her perspective. In times of fatigue and depression, I sometimes found myself revisiting the hurts Julie had caused me. Then, with God's help and an act of will, I decided to love and forgive and to share these struggles honestly with Julie so that we could support each other in the rebuilding of our relationship.

Because of the rumors spreading around town, we decided to explain to our two teenage children what had happened. We wanted them to hear it from us first and to know that we had made a decision to save our marriage. Our son and daughter were both shocked and hurt, and our son reacted with anger toward Julie that took several years to heal. To help defuse his hostility, we started written family dialogues once a week, which was a real turning point in rebuilding family unity. We had already joined another church, and both children went on a mission trip that brought them closer to each other and to God. Our daughter accepted Christ at this time, which helped her forgive her mother, although she, too, needed the help of counseling for a time to sort out her feelings and rebuild her relationship with Julie. Our son has forgiven her too, and we are reaping the dividends for our decision to keep our family together. Our daughter now says that the Marriage Encounter weekend was the best thing that ever happened to our family. For too long we had kept our feelings buried deep inside, and they were eating us up. Dialogue gave our family a way to communicate and to build a closeness greater than any of us thought possible.

Choosing to love and forgive was the toughest but most rewarding decision I ever made. Love is something for us to work at for the rest of our lives. Love means making time to communicate intimately with each other, taking walks together, attending and working on church functions together, parenting together. Love means being there for each other through better and worse. It has been many years now since our tragedy erupted, and we continue to love and grow in our relationship. There were times when we felt overwhelmed, hopeless, and weak, but God's love nurtured our smoldering wick back into a warm, healing flame.

ANONYMOUS

Reflection

1. What problems in your life have you avoided by "magical thinking," believing that you could pray them away without making any changes in your attitude and behavior?

2. What experiences have you had with receiving forgiveness and forgiving others? What attitudes make forgiveness possible? What attitudes get in the way?

In Sickness and in Health

Commentary

A husband's or wife's serious illness, chronic disease, or life-threatening injury changes life for the whole family. Dr. Wayne Sotile, author of *Heart Illness and Intimacy: How Caring Relationships Aid Recovery,* states that a couple facing such a situation may either strengthen their marriage and family life or erode their relationship by emotional distancing just when they are most in need of loving connection (pages xv–xvi). In his book (pages 250–52), Dr. Sotile encourages couples dealing with illness to develop and rehearse daily a healing philosophy based on statements such as the following:

1. We do not deserve this illness, but it has happened, bringing added pain to our lives.
2. What we do in reaction to this illness will either make the pain meaningful or allow it to destroy us as individuals and as a family.
3. It is all right for us to be angry about the situation, but it is not helpful to be angry at ourselves, at each other, or at God.
4. We need to pray for strength, determination, and willpower to cope, as well as for the grace to focus on what we still have, instead of what we have lost.
5. We will try to show each other how to live and love, despite our struggles.
6. Instead of asking why this illness happened to us, we will ask, "Now that this illness has happened, what can we do to cope, and who is available to help us?"
7. We affirm that we need each other and that we are grateful to be together.

My brothers and sisters, whenever you face trials of any kind, consider it nothing but joy, because you know that the testing of your faith produces endurance; and let endurance have its full effect, so that you may be mature and complete, lacking in nothing. JAMES 1:2-4

So we do not lose heart. Even though our outer nature is
wasting away, our inner nature is being renewed day by day.
2 CORINTHIANS 4:16

An Unexpected Challenge

I n the early 1980's, life seemed good. Our three children had grown up, and two of them had finished college and set out on their own. We looked forward to retirement, wondering if we would have any more adventures like those in our past. After eleven years as medical missionaries with The United Methodist Church in Liberia, West Africa, we had returned to New Hampshire. Bill now served as state health director, and I assisted students who had learning disabilities at the local junior-senior high school. Life was good, but sometimes we admitted to each other that it seemed a bit tame, compared with our years in Africa.

In 1985 all that changed. Bill, until then a healthy runner of races and marathons, learned that his symptoms were early indicators of Parkinson's disease. When the orthopedic doctor's matter-of-fact diagnosis was confirmed by a neurologist, we felt relieved that at least he did not have Lou Gehrig's disease, as did a close friend of ours. Although gradually debilitating, Parkinson's is not life threatening.

This neurological condition, which affects approximately one percent of the population over age sixty, is characterized by three major symptoms: tremors, rigidity, and slowness of movement. Related to these is a loss of balance with frequent falling. A deficiency of the chemical dopamine, which carries messages to the muscles and tells them when to move, causes these symptoms. Signs of Parkinson's disease usually are not noticeable until eighty percent of the brain cells that produce dopamine no longer do so. Since all muscle groups are affected, a flat and expressionless face, soft voice, slow movement, difficulty swallowing, and hesitant walking are all characteristic of Parkinson's patients. Treatment of the disease should be simple: just replace the missing dopamine. Unfortunately, it is much more complicated than that. Because Sinemet, the basic drug used in treatment, becomes less effective over time, other drugs must be used along with it. As the disease progresses, careful monitoring of the mix and timing of the drugs is required to allow optimal functioning.

We are a quiet couple, and we didn't really communicate about our feelings in regard to this major life event. Bill gradually slid into depression, while I distanced myself by becoming "as healthy as possible." *After all*, I thought, *I'm going to be the one in charge now.* This was a frightening, but mistaken, assumption. Fearing that Bill might lose his job if his diagnosis were known, we told only a few people outside our family, which prevented our receiving support and help from friends that might have made things easier. Whether or not we made the right decision to keep his illness a secret is debatable now.

We told our children, who were now living in other states, and sent them a book about Parkinson's. Our son, Bill III, sent his father a beautiful card expressing his love and admiration. Our middle child, Susan, told us later that she cried night after night, as did our youngest, Sandra. They questioned why God would allow this to happen to their dear dad. Our medical experience, however, had taught us that disease can come to anyone. We never asked why, but focused on how to deal with it.

As Bill's depression continued and deepened, he sought help. Because our faith has guided us through the years, he intentionally chose a pastoral counselor instead of a psychologist. This faith-based counseling helped him grapple with issues related to the disease and his future options.

As Bill's condition stabilized, we began reevaluating our life plan, asking, "What now, God?" Layoffs, downsizing, and lack of political support increased his frustration at work. I found my job more stressful as well. While considering possible job changes and moves to different locations, Bill asked God for five more years of work to allow us to develop adequate financial security for the future. In 1990, when we heard of an opening in West Virginia, Bill applied for and was hired as Commissioner of Public Health. He shared openly the fact of his illness, but the governor indicated that it would not be a problem as long as Bill could do the work. Relying on God's positive response to his prayer, Bill said he could probably plan on working for five more years.

Moving to Charleston proved a wise decision and a wonderful experience for both of us. God not only answered Bill's prayer but gave us a bonus year as well. His six years there turned out to be the most rewarding part of his public-health career. I chose not to take a paying job, but to participate in a number of volunteer activities, in order to be available if Bill needed my help.

We joined a large inner-city church, with a congregation made up mostly of older people. We both taught Sunday school classes and participated in DISCIPLE Bible study. I worked on mission outreach projects and in the activities of the women's organization. A newly founded Parkinson's disease support group provided us with a comfortable place where we could learn more about the disease and share our concerns.

As the years went by, Bill suffered increasingly from leg cramps and stiffness. Difficulty in adjusting his medications resulted in times when it was hard for him to function. Making allowances for these disruptions in his daily schedule was not always easy. Thanks to his wonderfully supportive staff, however, he continued to work until December of 1995. Bill then worked part-time until June of 1996, since the new commissioner was not available full-time until then. Several factors made this a difficult time: Bill's doctor, who had retired, referred him to a colleague with whom Bill could not establish a comfortable relationship; managing his medications became increasingly troublesome; and the looming threat of retirement, necessitated by the advancing of his disease, made him angry and depressed.

Bill went into therapy again, which was helpful. However, as his anxieties and strain increased, both his therapist and neurologist were often unavailable. With only each other to lean on, we experienced a deep sense of aloneness. Fortunately, we had both developed the practice of daily meditation in the form of the relaxation response, as in Herbert Benson's book by the same name. We read books by Dr. Gerald Mann, Henri Nouwen, and Bernie Siegel and deepened our spiritual life. Bill spent long hours in a chair, unable to read, watch television, or move much. During this time God's presence became very real to him.

I also sought counseling to help me deal with these changes. To my surprise, I learned that in trying to stay healthy myself, I had neglected to accept fully Bill's disease as part of my life. I could no longer avoid dealing with it. Realizing that I could not make things better for Bill, I could only stand by helplessly, keeping myself available in case he needed something. By writing out my frustrations and feelings and discussing them with my therapist, a sweet, cheery, and capable nun, I was able to regain strength and balance. After writing some poetry, I suggested Bill try his hand at it. He discovered a wonderful new talent and use for his "down times": composing poems and then later sharing them with others. God provided a new direction, which continues as a wonderful blessing for us.

During this time we invited our three children to spend a long weekend with us in order to discuss the disease, our expectations for the future, and ways they could be most helpful to us. We experienced a wonderful time of sharing, closeness, and reaffirmation of our mutual love and support.

When the new Commissioner of Public Health took over full-time, we wondered what to do next. Since we were not happy with the medical and psychological care Bill was receiving, and since no part-time job opening had materialized to keep us in West Virginia, we discussed the supports we would need and the best place to find appropriate professional care. After struggling for a while to understand where God was leading us, we decided to return to New England.

In September 1997, we bought a house just two doors down from our former home in New Hampshire, returning to our friends, neighbors, and church family of seven years before. The move itself, though stressful, proved a wise and positive one. Excellent medical and psychological care helped us both to stabilize. We appreciate being near Bill's mother, as well as my father and brother and his family. Our children visit and call regularly to check on us. Although there is no Parkinson's disease support group in this area, we plan to start one eventually. Perhaps as time goes on, Bill will find new ways to use his public-health knowledge and experience. I am already finding new outlets for my creativity.

Life is good. We've traveled a long and sometimes-frustrating way since Bill's diagnosis in 1985. It has not been an adventure we would have chosen, but it has been challenging and we have grown. Bill's disease will most certainly bring some hard times in the future, but God is good, and we know that together we can face whatever comes.

MARILYN AND BILL WALLACE
Bill and Marilyn live in Contoocook, New Hampshire.

Reflection

1. How did Bill and Marilyn's experience with disease and their understanding of life affect their adjustment to Bill's diagnosis?

2. What spiritual disciplines strengthened their faith and their ability to cope?

3. What beliefs do you hold and what disciplines do you practice that would help you cope with such a challenge?

> *Three times I appealed to the Lord about this, that it would leave me, but he said to me, "My grace is sufficient for you, for power is made perfect in weakness."*   2 CORINTHIANS 12:8-9a

The "Dis-ease" of a Disease

I somehow knew Keith was not joking, but I could not believe him when he said I was the one who had brought home the videos I found lying on our end table. He showed me my signature on the sheet from the video store; but no matter how hard I tried, I could not recall being there. Tears welled up in my eyes as I wondered what else I could not remember. A sense of dis-ease sweep through my soul. I knew something was wrong.

I had always taken pride in my excellent health. Now in my early forties, with two teenage daughters, I was in no way ready to accept illness as part of my life. Maybe I was imagining the continuing fatigue, constant pounding headaches, and the inconsistent double vision. Angry at what was happening to me and somehow believing that I could handle it alone, I tried to work even harder. Deep in denial, I spent longer hours at the office, as well as trying to keep a spotless house and be a perfect mother. But finally, six months later, no longer able to fool myself, I visited my doctor. Over the next four months, after numerous tests and consultations with various other doctors, the diagnosis came down: I had lupus, and it was centered in my central nervous system and brain. Treatment had to be aggressive and quick.

Sometimes treatment is as difficult to bear as the disease itself. First, prednisone was prescribed in large doses. Its initial side effect was mood swings so extreme that my family never knew how I would respond to them. Then this medication began to change my face and body. People I had known for years did not recognize me; when I tried to explain who I was and what was happening to me, they hurried on their way. I did not even know myself anymore: *Who was that person looking back at me in the mirror?* Both physically and emotionally, this disease had caused me terrible dis-ease.

When it became clear that the prednisone was not totally effective against my lupus, chemotherapy was prescribed. Fortunately, it did not include the ingredient that would cause me to lose my hair, but again I tried to handle things by myself. I felt so good right after the first treatment that I chose not to take the antinausea medication the hospital told me I needed. It took only one round of being violently ill all night to teach me a lesson!

I began to see that I was causing my own dis-ease by not admitting that lupus was changing my life forever. I had to accept the fact that I would not be able to do some of the things I had loved doing in the past. In fact, I might not even be able to remember some of those events that were so precious to my family and me. I needed their help to get through and out of the dis-ease of this disease.

Several years before I became ill, my husband participated in a Walk to Emmaus weekend and afterward insisted that I go too. As ordained clergy, we thought we understood about grace. The Walk to Emmaus, however, helped us understand grace, not just as a theological concept, but as a way of living. I had always thought I had to be perfect and hide any hurts—physical or emotional—I might have. Reflecting on my Emmaus experience now helps me to remember that God's grace is sufficient for me. I can share my incompleteness with others, including my family, and it is all right.

Keith is there through even the worst moments of this disease. From the day when all the tests began, through every single visit to the doctor, through all my ups and downs, he supports and loves me, in spite of how I might be acting or what I may be doing. He helps me to identify when I am doing too much, and sometimes he runs the sweeper at midnight so that I won't. He consoles me when the dis-ease seems overpowering. He encourages me to talk to a professional counselor so that I might come to terms with this illness and the changes it has brought to our lives.

The life we had planned together seems to have vanished, which is hard on Keith too. We can no longer go hiking or swimming at the beach on vacations. I have to avoid the sun or even bright florescent lights, and I have to be careful to avoid falling. I get depressed if I focus on what I cannot do.

A few months ago, when my lupus was very active, my doctor wanted me to consider taking disability leave. Keith and I cried and prayed, wondering how we could deal with this. With one daughter already in college and one a junior in high school, we were not certain how we could meet the challenge financially. Fortunately, my lupus went into remission, and I did not have to leave the work I love. But even more important is the fact that I chose not to be alone in this and allowed myself to share my fears and concerns with Keith.

One night while Keith was channel-surfing, we came across a television evangelist's healing service. Just at that moment, the speaker announced that someone was being healed of lupus. I don't doubt that God can heal, but healing comes in many different ways. For me, healing is letting go of whatever causes me to be ill at ease and coming to terms with the givens of this disease. I am learning to accept the reality of the lupus so that I can still have a full life.

Even though my lupus is in remission, I have to work to keep it there and to keep the accompanying arthritis under control. I have to pace myself, which sometimes means that I have to work at not working. Just recently, when we were all getting ready for trips and meetings, I got it in my mind that I needed to do all the laundry. "Who made you queen of the wash?" one of our daughters reprimanded me as she took the clothes basket out of my hands. God was so gracious to me in that, before I even knew why, I had accepted an appointment beyond the local church as director of a mission project. Little did I know how much I would need the flexible scheduling now available to me. I also had no idea how we all would need the love and support of the congregation Keith presently serves.

I do not know where God will lead. I continually ask God what is next, but Keith and I will know when we need to know. Until then, we will continue to support each other, so that this disease does not cause us the dis-ease of pain and confusion. Rather, the healing grace of Christ draws us closer to each other and to God.

RUTH AND KEITH SIMMONS

Ruth serves as director of Scott's Run Settlement House in Osage, West Virginia, and Keith serves as pastor of Woodland and Jones United Methodist Churches in nearby Morgantown.

Reflection

1. How have you experienced grace in your life?

2. When have you experienced the kind of healing Ruth describes as "coming to terms with the givens" of her disease?

Intervention

L ife with Roger had become unbearable. The marriage counselor, after listening to my story, declared that he thought Roger was an alcoholic and laid out a plan. First, he would counsel with me alone. Then, he would see our two sons and prepare us for an "intervention," a meeting during which we would all confront Roger with his behavior and insist on his entering a treatment program.

Steve, who had just graduated from high school and still lived at home, and Mark, in his early twenties and living about a hundred miles away, both agreed to participate, in spite of some doubts about how the plan would work. Throughout the months of our counseling sessions, Roger seemed completely unaware of any concerns. He worked hard both at his job and at clearing brush on the lot where we lived in a trailer and intended to build a new home as soon as possible. Roger always headed straight for the refrigerator after work and drank through the evening until bedtime. Steve and I stayed out of his way, trying to avoid triggering his outbursts of temper.

I had one friend I could talk to, but otherwise I carried this burden alone, along with our sons. I prayed constantly and felt that God directed me throughout. But by the time we held the intervention, I was drained and in a state of shock, close to a nervous breakdown. One day when we were coming home from a counseling session together, Mark and Steve expressed such discouragement that I pulled the car to the side of the road. We prayed desperately there together. I couldn't really talk to our pastor, although I loved him dearly. He always tried to smooth things over, and I knew that wasn't what I needed. I really didn't think anyone in our church would understand. My boss, however, was supportive. In addition to letting me leave work early for counseling sessions, he wrote a letter to get me excused from out-of-town jury duty for the week Roger was to come home from treatment.

The counselor preferred to schedule an intervention session during the day so that the client could go directly into the hospital's treatment program, which processes daytime admissions only. Because of Roger's and the boys' work schedules, however, we would have to meet in the evening, which meant Roger would have to come home for the night. The counselor insisted that one of the boys plan to drive Roger home and stay the night. He warned me to remove all weapons and medicine from the house first, since Roger might become violent or even suicidal. If necessary, I was to lock him out of the house. This was a scary prospect for me, but, fortunately, he did not react that way.

When the time came, I told Roger that I had been seeing a marriage counselor and that the counselor wanted to see him too. Roger was surprised to discover that I felt we had a problem, but he agreed to go. He was even more surprised when we got there and our two sons walked in together. That night, after the intervention, Roger couldn't sleep. He later told me that he tossed and turned and finally prayed, though he had never been much of a believer in prayer: "God help me. What am I going to do?" Suddenly calm, he slept after that and awoke in the morning still at peace, with no desire to drink. The treatment center kept him in detox an extra four days, waiting for him to experience some kind of withdrawal, but that never happened.

Although Roger actually seemed relieved to be in treatment, as if a weight had been lifted from his shoulders, I was so tired of this whole thing that at first I didn't even want to go visit him. Fortunately, I had begun attending Al-Anon meetings, even though I feared meeting people I knew there. Al-Anon encourages attending at least six times before giving up on the group; but Roger was in treatment by my sixth meeting, so I began attending the Al-Anon group at the hospital. I really needed the support.

After Roger entered the treatment program, Fred, one of his drinking buddies, came looking for him. He visited Roger and tried to talk him into leaving to get a beer. He told friends I was overreacting and tried to lay a guilt trip on me. "Roger drinks the way I do," he said. "Are you trying to say that I'm an alcoholic?" Fortunately, Roger was so clear about his situation that Fred's invitations didn't even tempt him.

After Roger came home, the treatment center recommended that we participate for two years in a couples group at a nearby counseling center.

At first I resented the thought of having to do yet one more thing for him, but I learned a lot during those two years. Some of the others yelled and screamed at each other, and some slipped back into drinking; but we actually began to communicate better. Roger's mind seemed sharper, and he helped more with making decisions. I told the boys, who both now lived elsewhere, that it was as if Roger had come back to life.

We really needed that couples group to help us cope with the difficulties we faced. The car engine blew, and then Roger lost his job. The company kept him on for a year after treatment, but one person, a self-righteous, self-proclaimed "born-again Christian," wrote Roger off as a sinner and kept engineering things to make him look bad. When Roger had a mild stroke the next summer, his medical expenses came out of the company's insurance, and they labeled him "high-risk." We had put all our savings into building our new home and had applied for a construction loan to finish the job. Roger was fired the same day we were to sign for the loan, but we got to the bank and signed the papers before the bank learned he was no longer employed.

Roger says it wasn't just losing his job that hurt; the impact on his self-esteem was even worse. He has always believed that you are what you do, and that you aren't much of a person if you don't have a job. Applying for jobs at age fifty-six is discouraging. He ended up working as a janitor, cleaning toilets and earning less than he could have drawn from unemployment compensation, but for him that was better than being on welfare. Fortunately, I still had my job, and the contractor let Roger do some of the work on our house, in order to reduce costs.

Looking back, we can see how alcoholism sneaked into our lives and gradually took control. Both of us grew up in Christian families, where we heard strong messages about the evils of alcohol. Before Roger entered military service, a friend of the family, who was a World War II veteran, took him out to bars, ostensibly to teach him how to drink. He bought Roger beers until he got sick. "Never again," Roger would say afterward, but by the next day he would be asking the friend when they could go again. During basic training and his tour of duty in Korea, an evening beer and occasional keg parties became routine for him. When he returned home, we married and he went back to school to train to be an aircraft mechanic. Alcohol took a back seat for a while, since I didn't drink at all and Roger felt that a mechanic should not take the risk of drinking.

A few years later, after Roger had left the airline company and had gone to work for an x-ray equipment firm, he hurt his back and could no longer lift. His company offered him a sales job in a neighboring state.

Roger commuted for several months before we moved to his sales territory. It wasn't until after his treatment program that I learned how frightened Roger had been during this transition. His small base salary made him dependent on earning good commissions. While commuting, Roger learned from other salesmen how to figure out which clients liked to drink, in order to entertain them at the company's expense. Lonely and afraid for his family's future, he drank in his room, then had drinks at dinner, then drank again in his room before bed. I had no idea this was going on. When we bought a new home, our former home did not sell for a while, and the prospect of having to pay two mortgages caused Roger to wake up in the night, terrified. His drinking escalated.

Over the next fifteen years, a slow progression took place. Roger's temper and behavior got worse. Neither of us had the background knowledge or understanding of alcoholism to realize what was happening. We continued in denial, keeping ourselves busy. I went to work when our youngest son started school. As the boys grew older, I worried about when they would leave home and would no longer be there to serve as a buffer between Roger and me. Once we went to a marriage enrichment weekend with friends from our church. We communicated better for a while after that and experienced some improvement in our relationship, but, as Roger puts it, "The alcohol was stronger than anything else."

When Roger went into treatment, people reacted with shock and surprise. We found out then who our real friends were. Of course, people who themselves live on the edge of alcoholism wanted nothing to do with us. Roger says he remembers how, when he was a trustee at the church, other members would talk about "those AA people." Such judgmental attitudes make it hard for people to recognize what is happening to them. Before we could get the help we all needed, we had to face the fact that Roger had a real sickness, over which he had no control. We thank God for guiding us through this process and for the wonderful, loving people who helped us heal!

ANONYMOUS

Reflection

1. Would people in your congregation feel ashamed to admit to an addiction? How might we create a church climate where people can acknowledge their struggles and ask for the help they need?

2. Denial plays a strong role in alcoholism and other addictions, as in many other personal difficulties. What weaknesses and vulnerabilities in your own life do you need to face?

To learn more about alcoholism, contact your local Alcoholics Anonymous or Al-Anon Family Group, or contact Al-Anon Family Group Headquarters, Inc., 1600 Corporate Landing Parkway, Virginia Beach, VA 23454-5617. Phone: 757-563-1600. Fax: 757-563-1655.
Internet (Al-Anon): **http://www.al-anon.alateen.org**
Internet (AA): **http://www.alcoholics-anonymous.org**

A Walking, Talking Miracle

The events of July 8, 1995, were the most frightening and most blessed of our lives. Lori took the children in our van to run errands while I drove the company truck in the other direction to get sand for the sandbox we planned to build that afternoon. On the way back, just as I pulled into the driveway, my pager beeped. I went inside to call and was told by the dispatcher that my family had been involved in an automobile accident and that I was needed at the hospital right away. I felt an adrenaline rush, the kind that just numbs you a bit. Hearing sirens, I ran out the door and jumped in my truck, reminding myself what a good driver Lori is. About eight hundred feet from our house, I came across a cluster of people and saw our van off the road, wrapped around a tree, its panels crumpled and windows shattered, smoke pouring out. Desperately I thought, *My family's gone.*

When I pulled to a stop, an officer I knew asked another man to get in the truck and told me to get to the hospital right away. I asked about my family, but he couldn't or wouldn't tell me anything except that Madeline, eleven months old at the time, was probably all right. He told me nothing about Lori, six-year-old Austin, or four-year-old McKenna. The trip to the Augusta hospital seemed to take forever. I prayed silently, but my mind raced, thinking of all the dreadful possibilities.

When I first arrived at the hospital, nobody could tell me anything. While I filled out forms, the nurse at the desk kept telling me that the doctors were still evaluating the situation, checking everyone's injuries. Then I heard a baby crying and knew it was Madeline. Running through the double doors, I found Lori's mother holding the baby. We embraced and wept together. The doctor told us that Maddy had no broken bones, but had a very sore face from the impact with her car seat.

At this point the chief surgeon on duty that day approached me. It was an act of God that this man, a semiretired neurosurgeon, was available, as all of Lori's injuries were neuro-related. He told me Austin was conscious, but had serious cuts on his face and was undergoing a CAT scan, because they feared he might have internal injuries. McKenna had been taken to another hospital about thirty miles away because she had so many injuries that they could not treat her in Augusta. As for Lori, he stated that she was in extremely critical condition, with severe head trauma. One of her eyes was fully dilated, indicating loss of brain function. He said few people ever recover from that. While I appreciated his honesty, his words left an empty feeling in the pit of my stomach. He further stated that her brain was swelling so rapidly that if she were to have any chance for survival, they needed immediately to begin treatment, a risky surgical procedure that involved coring a quarter-size hole in the skull plate, removing it, and placing a pressure-monitoring device right on the brain.

When I had signed the release for Lori's surgery and asked to see her, the doctor warned me about her appearance. On their way to the operating room, they stopped the gurney long enough for me and our pastor, who had just arrived, to pray over her. I was truly shocked by her appearance. She was covered with bruises and lacerations and was hooked up to a variety of tubes. As she was wheeled away, I was overwhelmed by the thought that I might never see her alive again.

Shortly after that, they told me Austin was back down in the emergency room. I found him looking both brave and scared at the same time as one of the doctors prepared to stitch up his facial cuts. I couldn't hug him because of his injuries, but I held his hand and just kept telling him how much I loved him. He kept asking about his mother, but I couldn't tell him anything. The doctor reported that the CAT scan showed that Austin had no internal injuries, but that he would have a very sore belly from the seat belt. I thanked God and continued to pray for Lori.

About an hour later, the doctor reported that Lori was out of surgery and back in recovery and that we would just have to wait to see how well the treatment would work. By this time, many of our Christian brothers and sisters had heard about the accident and had started praying for us; many showed up at the hospital. One of our dear friends spent three hours calling every Christian he knew to pray for us. There is nothing like the loving comfort of God's family in action.

Knowing there was nothing else I could do there, I headed for the other hospital to see McKenna. I felt guilty that she had been there all by herself for about six and a half hours. When I walked into her room in the ICU, our eyes met and we reached for each other, hugging and crying for about ten minutes. For the first time since I had been paged that morning, I felt a deep peace come over me; I knew it was going to be all right. I can't explain it, but I just knew that God was taking care of us. Medically, McKenna was fine, and they let her go the next morning. Because her spine had been compressed, she couldn't walk for a few days and we had to carry her everywhere, which she didn't mind at all.

Austin was discharged after two nights at the Augusta hospital. By then the doctor reported that Lori had responded well to the surgery, that her brain swelling had stabilized, but that she remained in extremely critical condition. He said that she would probably remain in a coma for two weeks, after which she would need months of rehabilitative therapy and would likely have permanent brain damage. I found these revelations sobering but not discouraging, because I was so thankful she was alive. Twice that day we held prayer circles around Lori's bed. Her healing from that point on was miraculous. To the amazement of the doctors, she regained consciousness later that day and was moved to a regular room. Two days later she was transferred to a rehabilitation center.

After evaluating her, the rehabilitation therapists predicted that she would be there for two weeks or maybe a month. At first Lori was frustrated; she knew something had happened, but couldn't understand what. I was stunned by the reality of her short-term memory loss. She would seem completely normal when we were talking, but moments later she would have forgotten what I had said. In five days, however, she was home. Again, she healed much more rapidly than anticipated. We called her our walking, talking miracle!

Lori later told me that she began to be aware of what was happening on her second day in rehab. Each morning the nurse put her in a wheelchair and sat her in front of the television for stimulation. On the second day, she remembered that happening the day before, and she could feel the weight of the injury on her brain being lifted. She says it felt like God's healing hands on her head, pulling the injury away. It took up to a year for everything to heal, but from that point on she started functioning again.

When we brought Lori home, we were struck again by evidence of God's incredible love: Flowers and cards were everywhere. People were weeding the garden, mowing the lawn, washing the dishes, and taking care of the children. God's love shone through them all around us. Lori paid one last joyful visit to her grandmother, who was dying but had been praying for Lori continually. We also heard from people who had experienced similar accidents and injuries, with whom we shared information about treatments and doctors.

In time we realized even more the blessings that had saved our children's lives. The fact that they were all in the back seats, properly strapped in, and sleeping when the car hit the tree certainly reduced the seriousness of their injuries. One of the rescue workers later told us of a blinding flash of white light he had experienced as he was pulling the children from the wreckage. We know that it was evidence of God's loving spirit protecting and helping them.

Lori's doctors determined that she had experienced a *petit mal* seizure and would not be allowed to drive again. I had to assume many responsibilities that next year while Lori continued to heal, and sometimes I felt as if I were caring for another child. Often I felt lonely, since she could not converse on a deep level for a while and was often preoccupied with her recovery and therapies. My gratitude that she and the children were alive and my happy memories of our relationship before the accident gave me patience and hope for the future.

And, of course, what we have now is even better. We don't let little things bother us anymore. We know there is goodness in life's trials, in the way we learn and in how our life changes. We were Christians before, but we tended to turn to Christ mostly when we needed him. Now we know how precious and fragile life is and what goodness God gives us every day. We both used to be independent and in control, but we have learned to receive help from others as a blessing, both for us and for those who give. Even death no longer frightens us, as we have grown closer to God and to each other through these events. I feel blessed to have my family back—as if I've been given a second chance. Unfortunately, we slip back into taking things for granted now and then; but remembering the miracle we have experienced, we cannot thank God enough for keeping us together here on earth a while longer.

SCOTT AND LORI MINOR

Scott and Lori live in Winthrop, Maine, where he works for the water district and she home-schools their children. Lori suffers some loss of peripheral vision and some memory problems, but otherwise has recovered well from the accident.

Reflection

1. Some studies report substantial proof of the healing power of prayer. What personal prayer habits and communities of prayer would you be able to call on in a crisis?

2. What does Scott mean when he calls this event "the most frightening and most blessed" of their lives?

> Above all, clothe yourselves with love, which binds everything together in perfect harmony. And let the peace of Christ rule in your hearts, to which indeed you were called in the one body. And be thankful.
> COLOSSIANS 3:14-15

"To Comprehend a Nectar"

I retired on December 31, 1993, when I was fifty-four and a half years old. Charlie had retired the previous June at fifty-nine. We had been married for thirty-two years, had raised four children, and had separated twice since the youngest had graduated from high school. We reconciled each time without really addressing the underlying issues, and the wounds had been encapsulated rather than healed, walled away so that the hurt wouldn't interfere with day-to-day living.

Even so, the previous two years had been quite good. We had both learned from age and experience to avoid "pushing each other's buttons," and we were blessed with wonderful children and friends and sufficient income to enjoy a comfortable life. On January 1, we left on a twelve-day trip to Florida to celebrate my retirement. We loved the climate there and reserved a condo for two months for the following winter. During the last few days of our trip, Charlie did not feel well, but we were still upbeat. After flying into Portland, we stopped for lunch in the Old Port before driving home, toasting each other and our "new life."

But Charlie felt worse each day, complaining of pain in his lower back. He went to see his doctor, a specialist in rheumatoid arthritis, an illness he had struggled with for many years. An MRI showed some arthritis in his spine, but not enough to account for what was now severe pain. Charlie had physical therapy to reduce the pain, but it didn't help. Each time he visited the doctor, he was questioned as to the exact location of the pain. On one visit, more in frustration than anything else, he said that he hurt everywhere, including his chest. The doctor ordered a round of more-comprehensive testing, including a routine visit to a cardiologist.

To us it certainly seemed routine. Charlie had never complained of any symptoms that I would have associated with heart problems. I sat in the waiting room during Charlie's stress test. Afterward, he came to get me, and we met with the cardiologist in his office. With no preliminary comments whatsoever, the cardiologist announced that Charlie's test showed blockages in the arteries leading to his heart and that he was scheduling a heart catheterization for the next week. Meanwhile, he prescribed a nitroglycerine patch for pain and sent us into the next room to watch a video on the process. We were too stunned to say much of anything.

Since the catheterization was billed as day surgery, we didn't bring anything with us to the hospital. When the procedure revealed severe blockages, the doctor decided to send Charlie directly by ambulance to the medical center in Portland, in order to beat an impending blizzard. I rushed home to pack for both Charlie and myself in case the weather kept me from returning home. I called a friend in Portland to see if I could stay with her; then I called the children and Charlie's brother.

On February 28, 1994, Charlie, still complaining about the pain in his back, had open-heart surgery, which went well. Although the surgery involved seven bypasses, we were elated that the problem had been discovered before he had a heart attack. Indeed, the surgeon said Charlie had the worst blockages he had ever seen in a patient who had not had a previous heart attack. Six days later we left the hospital. His recovery from surgery was routine and uneventful, but he still had the pain in his back.

The heart surgery turned out to be just a minor preliminary. The pain in Charlie's back got worse, and he began to spend time in bed curled up in a fetal position. More tests, more tests, and more tests were ordered. Finally, on May 19, 1994, the day Jackie Kennedy Onassis died of non-Hodgkins lymphoma, we received the biopsy results confirming the doctor's diagnosis of Charlie with the same disease. This time the diagnosis did not come as a shock, because the doctors had prepared us for that possibility. Our daughter-in-law had photocopied articles from medical journals, so I knew about the stages of the disease, as well as the statistics and the most successful treatments. Charlie never read any of the articles and did not want to know the statistics. He just lived each day and didn't try to look into the future.

After a trip to the Dana-Farber Clinic in Boston for consultation, we began chemotherapy the first week in June. I say "we" because it felt as if both of us were going through it. We were both so afraid of chemotherapy that we expected a dreadful reaction the minute the needle was inserted, but nothing really happened, other than the predicted bad taste in his mouth. He got up and walked out of the office, and we both marveled at his being alive. Indeed, within two weeks the terrible pain was much reduced, and Charlie began to talk of going to our cottage in Nova Scotia for a vacation.

For the next two years, we experienced a cycle of chemotherapy, wait, test, hope, relapse, more chemotherapy, wait, test, hope, relapse. And then in October of 1996, despite Charlie's history of seven bypasses and the fact that at sixty-two he was pushing the upper age limit, he entered the hospital for a bone-marrow transplant. During the frightening twenty-eight days required for this procedure, I spent at least six hours at the hospital every day, in addition to the hundred-mile roundtrip drive from our home. Fortunately, support from our friends and family carried us through. We never felt alone. Since then Charlie has steadily gained strength. Although there is a fifty-percent chance of relapse, we are basically living the life we had planned to live, but enjoying it more deeply.

Several days before Charlie entered the hospital for the transplant, we had a healing service at home. This service used to be called "receiving the last sacrament" (or the last rites), but the Catholic Church has broadened it to include an emphasis on healing. A dear friend of ours who is a retired priest led the service, during which Charlie and I both received the sacrament as a symbol of what we were facing. Our children and special friends were with us. One of those friends was actively battling cancer at the time and has since died. Another has been diagnosed recently with cancer too.

In many ways, facing the combination of heart surgery and cancer provided a real healing experience for us mentally, emotionally, and spiritually. It certainly gave us a different perspective on what's really important. Emily Dickinson said it well when she wrote: "To comprehend a nectar requires sorest need." No matter how many times you hear people say that you should enjoy every moment of life to the fullest, you don't realize what that means until you face death. You don't really know what a good time is until you discover how blessed it is to be without pain. A day spent without having to discuss symptoms is a wonderful gift for which we thank God. Just getting up in the morning, enjoying our meals, and conversing with friends are blessings we deeply appreciate.

This changed perspective makes it easier for us to accept those inevitable differences in temperament and style that used to be so problematic for us. What we went through changed us as individuals, making us more relaxed and grateful and more accepting of each other's foibles. That change has strengthened our marriage.

Charlie and I have both been administrators all our professional lives, and we both have a terrible tendency to see things as best organized in a certain way, often not the same way. We've learned, however, that harmony is more important than good organization. Because of all the years and the various crises we've faced and lived through, we have developed better methods of communication. Even more important, we've developed the willingness to stop before escalating a difference of opinion into an argument. We've learned that when a married couple fights, no one wins unless both win. We thank God for that discovery and for the chance to live together out of that new understanding.

CYNTHIA AND CHARLES TANOUS

Charles and Cynthia, both retired school administrators, live in North Turner, Maine. Cynthia is president and Charlie is the business manager of Educational Skills, Inc., a nonprofit organization that manages grants and conducts third-party evaluations.

Reflection

1. Wayne and Mary Sotile, in *Supercouple Syndrome: How Overworked Couples Can Beat Stress Together,* note that the coping strategies that foster success in our work may significantly interfere with our ability to maintain loving relationships. Coping skills that help us on the job include the following: ability to work hard and relentlessly, capacity for doing and/or thinking more than one thing at a time, competitiveness, desire for control, perfectionism, and the tendency to go numb under stress and keep on going (page 9). The skills that lead to successful and fulfilling relationships, on the other hand, are those that allow us to connect. These include the ability to slow down and pay attention to those around us, the ability to focus intently on the thoughts and feelings of another person, and the willingness to feel and communicate our own emotions and to allow others to do the same (page 96). Which of the above work habits and attitudes interfere with your relationships?

2. What choices could you make to help yourself slow down, pay attention to others, reveal more of who you really are, and nurture those you love?

Until We Are Parted by Death

Commentary

When I was about twelve years old, I found a yellowed scrap of newsprint tucked in a book in my grandfather's library. To this day I remember the words that so poignantly expressed what my stoic, New England grandfather could not speak about the death of his wife some years earlier: "And the stately ships go on to their haven under the hill; but oh for the touch of a vanished hand, and the sound of the voice that is still" (Alfred Lord Tennyson, "Break, Break, Break," 1842).

How do we prepare ourselves for death—either our own or of those we love—for that final and mysterious separation? Even if we share the faith of the Mexican pastor who bid me farewell with twinkling eyes, "Till we meet again, if not in this world, then in the next," death brings to an end this life's shared joys and struggles. The challenge for us is to live each day so that what we have built together will strengthen and bless whoever is left behind.

When death is swift and unexpected, spouses and families often find themselves in shock, regretting missed opportunities to express love and care for the one who is now gone. Those suffering through terminal illness experience the tension between wanting the suffering to end and wanting to cling to whatever they have left. Standing by someone who is dying to affirm that he or she is a unique and beloved child of God is a sacred task. In the following story, you will see how one couple shared the long journey through illness to death, allowing suffering to transform them in a way that blessed their family, friends, and community.

In my Father's house there are many dwelling places. If it were not so, would I have told you that I go to prepare a place for you? And if I go and prepare a place for you, I will come again and will take you to myself, so that where I am, there you may be also.

JOHN 14:2-3

Life Quake

On a day in August of 1993, the ground moved for us. We had come to Mercy Hospital in Portland, Maine, for a CAT scan to determine if the recently detected cancer in Arlene's colon had spread elsewhere. The ground moved when a technician reported that the radiologist had requested another test that would give a closer look at her liver. The technician, reading the alarm on our faces, assured us, "Oh, this test is painless; no need to be concerned."

Arlene replied, "I'm not worried about the procedure, but what it might reveal."

I think we already knew that the news would not be good. Questions, prayers, and fleeting thoughts raced through my mind: *Why? Why her? Why now?* Most of my prayers were really groans and sighs, which the Scriptures tell us God understands. Among my fleeting thoughts flashed memories of our life together through forty years of marriage and of our family, along with recollections of the meaning and the love we had experienced together. *Well,* I thought, *perhaps the "why" questions should be applied to the blessings as well.*

A few days later, after Arlene's surgery, we learned that the cancer had broken through her intestinal wall and entered the lymph system, which meant it was in her blood. The surgeon also confirmed fourth-stage malignancy in her liver. There is no fifth stage. The ground still shook for us with the tremors that had begun with the testing.

How does one deal with stage-four cancer? A team of doctors, after some discussion, decided to offer treatment and assigned Arlene, with her consent, to an oncologist. Each day in this process unfolded more knowledge of the situation and new insight about the process of treatment, new hopes and new fears. After a few weeks of recovery from the surgery, Arlene started chemotherapy treatments with 5-FU, an old and somewhat effective cancer-treatment drug.

From the beginning, the oncologist spoke in a straightforward manner. After examining her, he said, "Arlene, your cancer is incurable, but we will hold you as long as we can with this drug. Eventually, the cancer will win." These were hard words to hear, even though we already knew the extent of the disease. It took time for such grim news to sink into our understanding. What felt like the movement of the ground beneath us was really the quaking of our very lives!

The routine of her treatments, varying from time to time because of the many side effects from the medications, became a major focus for us during the next three years. The side effects necessitated other medications, and each new medication pushed the reality of the cancer at both of us. We adapted to the incessant and tiring routine, and even found a sense of security during the treatments. Although her two- or three-week breaks from treatment were experienced as times of liberation, we worried then that the cancer might be spreading.

Arlene rose to meet this challenge with great resiliency, and I served as her companion during the weekly treatments as well as her visits to other doctors between her cancer-treatment appointments. There were only four times when my schedule as a local church pastor kept me from accompanying her. We felt truly together in this. In late September we attended a Discovery weekend, which was a good experience for both of us. We gained more information about cancer and interacted with other support people and cancer patients, some recently diagnosed and others longer-term survivors. This event helped us focus on the realities of our situation and encouraged us in the direction of hope. Our daughter Judi attended another session in May, when her mother participated on a panel of those telling their stories.

The skills we had learned through participating in and leading marriage enrichment events during the past twenty years served us well throughout all that we now had to face. Present circumstances called upon us to be doers of that which we had learned and taught in less-stressful times. Sharing honestly at the feeling level made it possible for us to help each other through the hard times ahead.

We determined not to function out of a mindset of "battling" cancer, although it was indeed a battle most of the time. We chose to take a stance of "seeking to live with" cancer. It was an uninvited guest in our relationship, but it was very real and very present. Years ago, when our children were young, we chose a symbol and a message that we painted on the freezer that stood in our kitchen. The message, "Life is struggle.... Dance!" was illustrated by a painting of Snoopy, the cartoon dog, in his famous dancing pose, complete with top hat and cane. We had hoped that this image would bring us courage and hope in the midst of life's struggles. Could we still respond so positively now that cancer had joined us in the dance?

The reality of cancer focused our attention on two challenges: coping with the effects of this life-threatening disease on her body and contemplating the meaning of life (sorting out what is important from what is trivial). We were jolted into a deepened awareness that life must be lived in the here and now, receiving our time and space and relationships as precious gifts from God. We found ourselves welcoming each new day less routinely and more as a miracle, a realization often challenging and at the same time consoling and healing. Facing this life-threatening reality, we chose life and the life dance, and we tried to live each day we had together to the fullest.

We began to see more clearly and to focus more intently. Our family relationships deepened. We looked lovingly into the eyes of our friends with a deepened gratitude. We savored sights and the sounds of music. We took walks and bike rides as often as Arlene's energy level would allow. As we strolled along a beach near our home, the waves and tides reminded us of life's rhythms, to which one could dare to dance. The sunsets along the oceanfront fed our souls with the beauty and mystery of the gifts of creation. Even as she lovingly urged me to remarry someday, we set out to cherish together every minute of time she had left on this earthly trek.

Most days this worked well for us. To look at Arlene, you would not have guessed that she was ill, which perhaps made it hard for those around her to accept her illness. She often said, "I wish I felt as good as people say I look!" After surgery she had to give up her work at Gorham Savings Bank, which she had loved. She did return to directing the church choir for another year and continued on with some of her piano students. Although fatigue would get the best of her at times, she persisted with her letter writing, church activities, and homemaking. I gave as much assistance as I thought she would tolerate: shopping, cleaning, cooking—even general dusting and laundry. She sometimes said to me, "Don't take this over yet. There will be a time when you will have to, but not yet. I have given up so much already."

Arlene had a recurring dream in which friends, members of our church, or colleagues from her workplace would walk up to her and give her their watches. Sometimes people would take clocks off the walls and give them to her, or she would open a package and find a clock. She knew people were praying for her to have more time, and she often said, "People are praying for a miracle, but it has already happened. I have had a wonderful life and more time than I first thought I would have after the diagnosis."

Arlene journaled and kept copious notes in her date books throughout the years of our marriage, often speaking of someday writing the family history. Now was the time to get it done. She organized that material, typed it into the computer, and edited it to her satisfaction. In addition, we took time to focus on each of our five children and brainstormed all we could remember about them. She typed up and edited that material as well. Next we sorted through hundreds of pictures, preparing a pictorial history of each child, which we organized into scrapbooks and presented to them for Christmas, 1995.

We had discussed our long-range goals many times: retiring, buying our first home, and settling into the retirement years together. We had dreamed of doing more traveling, since we had already enjoyed a number of interesting and educationally stimulating trips. Now we were thankful that we had said *yes* to those opportunities throughout our marriage and had not put them off until those magic "retirement years." In October, with a deep sense of prayer discernment, we decided that I would take early retirement in June of 1996, accelerating our previous plans by two years. We contacted a realtor and prayed for God's guidance in the process of buying a home. Doing this together gave me a great sense of satisfaction, since the thought of having to decide alone where to live in retirement left me with feelings of emptiness and fear. We had fun making the decision together, choosing a townhouse in Scarborough, Maine, and working together to make this living space comfortable—filled with mementos of our life together and now brimming over with meaning for me.

We moved not one day too soon, for in the summer Arlene's condition began to change. The cancer was gaining ground. Radiation therapy to reduce a sizable tumor in her liver seemed to work for a few weeks, but the advance continued. Our oncologist administered a newly released drug that he thought would be less toxic than the one she was taking. However, after five treatments, discouraged by her loss of hair, heavy nausea, and unbearable fatigue, we decided to stop the treatments. She wanted her remaining days to have as much quality as possible. Her doctors did not protest this decision.

About this time, her discomfort began to increase to the extent that milder pain medications no longer helped. She was introduced to morphine, beginning with oral doses but soon switching to an intravenous pump through her *med-a-port*, a tube that had been implanted near her shoulder for her chemotherapy. The cancer continued to advance, surrounding and closing off the bile duct and causing her to be hospitalized for ten days in December. A surgeon inserted a stent in the duct, which held for several weeks, but the cancer grew above the stent and began to shut down her liver function once again.

This was a particularly hard Christmas season for us, knowing it would be her last and wanting to savor each moment. She had always put the final decorations on our tree, but did not have a chance to do that because of her hospital stay. When I took down the tree, she asked if I would bring the decorations to her. Most of them were gifts from friends over the past forty years, and many were made or given by our children. She wanted to touch them and pack them up for the last time, which she did in a careful and loving fashion.

After Christmas, her pain increased, necessitating additional medication. Hospice nurses, whose visits increased from once a week to once a day over an eight-week period, carefully monitored this process, trying to balance her comfort needs with her strong desire to remain lucid and communicative. She remained at home during these last weeks of her life, content to be in our own space and surrounded by loving family and a host of friends.

Throughout the forty-two years I had known Arlene, we had always shared our hopes and dreams, our frustrations and our fears. We had grown in our relationship so that we knew how to share with each other at a deep level. We had learned to listen carefully to each other, and from that listening came a sensitivity and caring that deepened the love in our relationship and brought strength and stability. We needed all we could muster for the days ahead.

Each morning throughout her illness she got up, dressed herself, and prepared for the day. On Friday, February 28, she felt weak and unstable, not sure that her legs could support her. Her strength improved some the next day, so she was able to get up with some help and the support of a walker. We decided on Monday to order a hospital bed, which was placed in the dining room on the first floor, where she would be in the center of family activity. Jim and his wife, Debra, Chris and his wife, Jennifer, and Judi were already with us. On Thursday, Andy and Susan arrived, completing the circle. Arlene's brother Richard also came by.

At the beginning of the week, she said to me one morning, "I think this is it."

I responded, "Honey, I believe you are right." We held each other close in a silent and tearful embrace, feeling the urgency of these final days of love and friendship. Throughout the week, friends stopped by, and she asked me to call her mother and father, other family members not present, and a few friends so that she could speak to them and say good-bye. Some did not realize until after the fact that she was indeed saying farewell, although she was forthright and brave. I had been watching her gradually give up so many of the activities and projects that had brought her satisfaction. It was painful to watch this happen, but we were able to talk about the process and the pain. Now we were down to that which she cherished the most: her relationships with people. How she loved her family and her friends!

It was a great comfort to both of us to have our children present. On Thursday evening about ten, she asked us all to gather around her bed. All through the years, the table had served as a significant gathering place for our family. Now she likened this circle around her bed to being "around the table." The symbolism seemed most appropriate.

She spoke a personal word to each of the children: Looking each one in the eyes and speaking as if no one else were in the room, she told them how much they meant to her, how much she loved each of them. Then she spoke to them collectively, admonishing them to always follow the cross. Softly she said, "I am the cross." When we look at the cross, we see suffering and love; when we looked at her, we indeed saw suffering and love. I felt her desire for them to make that connection. In conclusion, she asked a question: "Where is the church?" She then answered with the refrain of the Avery and Marsh hymn "We Are the Church." The children had learned those words as youngsters and said them along with her. She then began singing the chorus of "I Need Thee Every Hour," and we joined her in those prayerful words.

At two in the morning she asked for me. I had left the room for some rest about forty-five minutes earlier; but we had a pact, the children and I, that if there were any change, all were to be awakened. When I joined her, an extraordinary happening took place. Grasping my hands, she lifted them into the air and said, as though she were introducing me to someone, "This is my loving husband." She spoke other words out of the depth of our love, kissed my hands all over and held them close to her.

That was the last time she related to any of us, except for brief words spoken to whoever was sitting beside the bed when she roused. She spoke of crowds along the road ahead and of feeling affirmed. As she looked toward the adjoining living room, she spoke of light and brightness: "Some may say that is only the curtains, but I see angels." She spoke of seeing a little girl in a black coat. And then she spoke of a baby and asked who was going to take care of the baby. Another time she said, "Sing? Why, I have been singing all my life!" Indeed, she had.

On Monday, March 3, she continued in pain, but medication kept her fairly comfortable, and she did not stir much throughout the day. By evening her breathing had changed, with rattling sounds and efforts to cough. She arched back her head, probably trying to ease her breathing. I moved closer, placed my right hand under her neck and head and my left hand on her shoulder. I began to whisper in her ear how much I loved her and that I would always carry her in my heart, that I would never forget her. She had been my best friend, my companion, my lover, my soul mate, the mother of our children, the one who brought meaning and music into our relationship.

As I spoke, her neck eased, her head relaxed from its rigid position, and her breathing became less labored. She gave two pushes, much like those we had practiced together in Lamaze training, as if she were giving birth to her soul. Then it was over. She was no longer with us. We said our farewells in the weighted silence that filled the room, heavy with the mysteries of life and death.

One of the children pointed out to me that the music had stopped. We had played CDs throughout the week, noting how she smiled to hear her favorite pieces, even though resting with her eyes closed. The final song on this CD was a magnificent version of the hymn "Old Hundredth Psalm Tune," which ended with an interlude followed by an Amen. Arlene had died during the interlude before the final Amen of that great hymn of praise. How fitting for one whose soul had been touched by music at an early age, and for whom sacred music nurtured her spirit. No wonder the silence felt so heavy.

During the week I had noticed a rebonding taking place among our children, who had not been together in our home for some years. I was also mindful of the importance of supportive community throughout those days. Visitors rang our doorbell, goodies in hand, expressing their love and concern in the only way they could. Others called or wrote, often simply affirming, "We are holding you in prayer." Several spoke of the love they felt as they entered our home. Even the nurses who had cared for Arlene tarried, entered into conversations, and became a part of the family, even if for a moment. These contacts were significant and important, reminding us of how many friends and colleagues were there for us, even in this most difficult time.

A competent and wonderful woman, Arlene had remained strong in spirit while her body was growing weaker. For several months she had worked with a good friend, also a pastor, talking through her death and planning her memorial service. She cared for every detail, even to the point of personally asking each of those who were to participate in the leadership of that service. One of the many letters I received after her death said this: "Thank you for providing us all with a wonderful celebration of Arlene's life and ministry. Our family learned so much from yours last Saturday about living and dying as disciples of Jesus Christ. Remembering Arlene and learning from her was a priceless gift."

And so it was and is! Although I struggle with loneliness as I try to adjust to my new reality, my heart is filled with gratitude for all that we shared and for the continuing power of our love.

RICHARD M. HAMILTON

Richard is a United Methodist pastor, now retired from the New England Conference but serving a part-time pastorate in Maine.

Reflection

1. Our culture has been criticized for its denial of death. What was your first experience with the death of someone you knew or of someone close to you? What attitudes toward death did you learn growing up? How have your attitudes and feelings changed?

2. If you knew that you were close to death, what would you want to say to your spouse? children? parents? significant others?

3. It is easier to deal with such matters as wills, funeral and burial arrangements, and other final wishes when death is not apparently imminent. What arrangements have you and your spouse already made for your eventual deaths? What do you need to take care of or discuss?

4. If you were to take seriously the challenge in this story to live life "in the here and now, receiving our time and space and relationships as precious gifts from God," what would you do differently?

Two excellent resources for people dealing with death and dying are listed on page 120.

Building Strong Relationships

Commentary

In the midst of difficult times, it is often hard to imagine that we will ever be joyful again. The stories in this book, however, bear witness to the reality of God's transforming presence and power, even in our most painful and frightening experiences. These couples affirm that on the other side of struggle, suffering, and trauma, it is possible to find even greater happiness than was known before. Indeed, "weeping may linger for the night, but joy comes with the morning" (Psalm 30:5b).

These stories also illustrate coping and relationship skills that can enhance our personal growth and our ability to deal with whatever challenges life may offer. It is hoped that the "Reflection" questions accompanying each story will help you identify your own issues and prompt you to consider your own needs for growth. The following "Toolbox" pages (pages 97–102) elaborate on some of these skills and suggest specific strategies for learning and developing them.

Many couples find that meeting with others who have similar experiences and needs is one of the most effective ways to strengthen their marriages. The leader's guide in this section (pages 103–15) provides an easy-to-follow plan for using this book in a small-group setting.

Many other good resources are available to help couples enhance their relationships. Those listed in "Sources" (pages 116–17) and "Resources for Further Help" (pages 118–20) provide an excellent starting point.

Therefore, since we are surrounded by so great a cloud of witnesses, let us also lay aside every weight and the sin that clings so closely, and let us run with perseverance the race that is set before us, looking to Jesus the pioneer and perfecter of our faith, who for the sake of the joy that was set before him endured the cross, disregarding its shame, and has taken his seat at the right hand of the throne of God.   HEBREWS 12:1-2

Toolbox: Communicating Feelings

Although emotions offer important clues about what is going on within us as individuals or in our relationships, we may have difficulty acknowledging them because of beliefs about what we should or shouldn't feel. Repressed feelings can control us and trigger destructive behaviors. If we deny our negative feelings, we are also likely to have difficulty getting in touch with and expressing positive ones.

It isn't helpful to dump our feelings on others or to use our feelings as weapons. Expressing them nondefensively, however, frees us from their power. In addition, such communication gives others important information about our needs and about how they can relate to us most helpfully. "Speaking the truth in love" (Ephesians 4:15) is vital both for our own mental and spiritual well-being and for the health of our relationships.

We can communicate emotions most effectively by describing them in a sentence beginning with the words "I feel...." At this point, if someone kindly says, "Tell me about it," we sense that we have permission to proceed with more detail. Blaming others for our feelings usually puts them on the defensive. Clearly describing the circumstances will more likely elicit understanding and support. (For example, "I feel frustrated when I have to clean up the kitchen all by myself after all the work of preparing the meal.")

The listener can demonstrate understanding of what has been said by providing reflective and empathic feedback: "You are probably tired and don't feel that it's fair for you to have to do so much of the work around here." When the listener reflects back possible underlying feelings, the speaker feels understood or can correct the listener's perception, if necessary. The listener, of course, will also need opportunity to share feelings, but should not try to do so until the speaker feels she or he has been heard. "If one gives answer before hearing, it is folly and shame" (Proverbs 18:13).

Dr. Thomas Gordon describes these strategies, called "I-messages" and "active listening," in his book *Parent Effectiveness Training: The "No-Lose" Program for Raising Responsible Children* (pages 49–53 and 115–20). Most relationship programs include some variation of this process. For example, in *A Lasting Promise: A Christian Guide to Fighting for Your Marriage* (pages 59–69), couples are instructed to practice a "speaker-listener technique," in which they actually pass an object back and forth to clarify whose turn it is to share feelings.

Toolbox: Negotiating Solutions

Too often we try to resolve problems in such a way that either "I win and you lose" or "you win and I lose." The following five-step method can help couples find solutions acceptable to both by treating each other as equals, with the needs of both parties receiving like consideration. Joint ownership of both the problem and the solution increases the couple's commitment to make their plan work, "united in the same mind and the same purpose" (1 Corinthians 1:10b).

1. Each person shares fully his or her feelings and needs in regard to the stated topic. While one is sharing, the other listens carefully, responding with reflective statements: "I hear you saying that…," "You need…," or "You would like…". (If necessary, review "Toolbox: Communicating Feelings," on page 97.)
2. When both parties agree that they have shared all the feelings and needs of which they are aware, they take a blank sheet of paper and brainstorm all the solutions they can think of for the stated problem. Every idea should be written down without evaluation, since expressing negative reactions would limit the flow of creative ideas. Both parties should feel free to offer "far-out" or even absurd suggestions, because they could trigger other ideas that might work.
3. After an extensive list has been drafted, each party crosses off any ideas that are unacceptable to him or her.
4. From the remaining items on the list, the parties agree on one that they are willing to try, negotiating who will do what, when, and where. They should also agree on a target date for evaluating how well the chosen solution is working and for renegotiating the plan, if necessary.
5. If there are no items left on the list after Step 3, further sharing of feelings will be needed before attempting to brainstorm again. Some problems require extensive negotiation over long periods of time.

This process, based on Dr. Thomas Gordon's "no-lose" method presented in *Parent Effectiveness Training: The "No-Lose" Program for Raising Responsible Children* (pages 236–42), is developed in greater detail in the book *A Lasting Promise: A Christian Guide to Fighting for Your Marriage* (pages 71–82).

Toolbox:
Two Ways to Improve a Marriage

The purpose of marriage enrichment is to make good marriages better, but it is not a substitute for therapy. Here are some guidelines to help couples determine which is appropriate for them.

Enrichment	Counseling
1. Couples want to face whatever is unsettling in their relationship. They believe they have potential for growth.	1. Couples sense that something is wrong with their marriage, but they avoid facing it.
2. They can identify the problem(s) and agree about what they want to work on.	2. They have difficulty identifying the problem or agreeing what to work on.
3. They believe they have enough positives going for them to make their marriage worth some effort.	3. They feel overwhelmed by the negatives in their relationship. One or both may feel like giving up.
4. They can talk about their problems and are open to learning new skills for dealing with issues.	4. They find their problems too painful to talk about.
5. Focusing on their relationship fosters growth and development.	5. Focusing on their relationship makes matters worse.
6. They may have anger, but they are not consumed by it.	6. They are so angry with each other that they cannot focus on the problem without hurting each other.

For a qualified marital therapist, consult The American Association for Marital and Family Therapy website (**http://www.aamft.org**). Contact information for various marriage enrichment programs are listed on pages 118–20.

• • •

Based on an article by Antoinette and Leon Smith for *The Association for Couples in Marriage Enrichment Newsletter*, Volume 17, Number 7, July–August 1989. Used by permission.

Toolbox:
Managing Anger

David and Vera Mace, in *How to Have a Happy Marriage: A Step-by-Step Guide to an Enriched Relationship*, state that anger, a normal human emotion, can be a powerful tool for personal growth and for increasing intimacy and marital satisfaction. Anger, like pain, is an important cue that something is wrong and needs to be addressed. Sometimes anger is a secondary emotion, occurring as a result of underlying loneliness, fear, or other feelings a person might not want to admit. Dialoguing about anger by using "I-messages" and "active listening" can help couples get to the underlying feeling.

In their book (pages 111–15), the Maces suggest the following three-step process for dealing with anger:

Step 1: We agree to tell each other about our anger as soon as we become aware of it. Since we accept without question our right to be angry, no shame is implied by revealing it.

Step 2: We determine not to attack or hurt each other with our anger. We try simply to communicate the state of our emotions, without accusation or blame.

Step 3: We ask for each other's help in dealing with any anger that develops, whatever the cause.

How well we are able to follow this process will depend in part on what we learned about anger in our families of origin. Those of us who were taught while growing up that nice people do not get angry have to unlearn that idea and practice clarifying our thoughts and feelings in order to communicate our needs. As it says in the Book of Ephesians: "Be angry but do not sin; do not let the sun go down on your anger, and do not make room for the devil" (4:26-27).

Two other helpful resources for understanding anger and learning how to manage it are Harriet Lerner's *The Dance of Anger: A Woman's Guide to Changing the Patterns of Intimate Relationships* and David Mace's *Love and Anger in Marriage*.

Toolbox:
Nurturing Spiritual Growth

Spirituality involves both our attitude toward God and our willingness to be guided in our daily lives by the values and teachings of our faith. Spirituality is intensely personal, and the extent to which couples share easily in this area depends largely on their experiences and individual spiritual styles. Individuals differ in what they find helpful to their spiritual growth, and couples will not always be at the same place in their faith journeys. We can, however, seek to honor, understand, and encourage each other's spiritual growth.

Communities of faith provide various opportunities for nurturing spirituality. Some people respond to celebrative worship and inspiring sermons, while others respond to Bible study and discussion groups. Some thrive in prayer groups, while others draw closer to God by participating in mission and service projects (*Team Spirituality: A Guide for Staff and Church*, by William J. Carter; pages 134, 138). Couples may share in such activities or may need to support each other's differing needs and interests.

We may also nurture our connection with God by weaving a variety of intentional practices into our everyday lives: table grace, formal prayers and use of devotional materials, morning prayers (thanks for the night's rest and requests for guidance during the day), evening prayers (expressing gratitude for the day's blessings and letting go of worries and disappointments), intercessory prayers for loved ones and for those with special needs, quiet moments of attentiveness to God, speaking and listening to God during daily activities, meditation, breath prayers, hymns, and Scripture passages. All of these, practiced either together or alone, nurture spirituality, which in turn shapes our attitudes and behavior and strengthens us for coping with the events of our lives.

Howard and Charlotte Clinebell define spiritual intimacy as the way couples share in matters related to ultimate concerns, the meaning of life, and their relationship to God and the universe (*The Intimate Marriage*, page 31). Participating together in faith-based groups or private spiritual disciplines enriches us, both individually and as a couple. Telling each other about our conversations with God—convictions, joys, doubts, frustrations, and struggles—helps us grow, increases our mutual understanding, and encourages us to pray more meaningfully for each other. As it says in the Book of James: "Draw near to God, and he will draw near to you" (4:8a).

Toolbox:
Nurturing and Protecting Your Love

As couples settle into marriage, most experience a period of disillusionment, during which they struggle to change each other, sometimes fearing they may have married the wrong person. Healthy couples mature by accepting their individual differences and the limitations inherent in any relationship. For couples who do not achieve this stage of differentiation and who do not learn effective ways to solicit what they want from each other, discontent may deepen into resentment.

In many cases of infidelity, wandering spouses seek something they think is missing in their marriage, perhaps the spark that was there initially but which is now buried under the debris of daily living. If unfaithful spouses invested in their marriages the same energy they put into affairs, or if they could develop effective communication and conflict-management skills, they might find what they are seeking in their own back yards. Unfortunately, it is too easy to think that the grass is greener on the other side of the fence, focusing on what someone else appears to offer and overlooking the negatives about him or her, as well as overlooking what you already have—or could have—in your marriage. Scott Stanley, in *The Heart of Commitment*, emphasizes the importance of pulling away from tempting relationships and firming up boundaries, in order to protect your marriage. He also cautions that it is equally important to work to reinforce the marriage relationship, which means giving priority to behaviors that strengthen the bond between you: expressing appreciation, having fun together, touching, sharing hopes and fears, and connecting spiritually (pages 55–65).

Because attraction to someone other than your mate is a such a common experience, every couple should develop a plan for what they will do if that occurs. If they agree to be honest with each other and to accept such attractions as normal but dangerous, they can then ask each other for the help they need to stay faithful. Couples who treat their love as a treasure to be guarded (or as a beautiful garden to be nurtured and protected), and who support each other's individual growth while maintaining an intimate connection, will reap the reward of a lasting, fulfilling life together.

Leader's Guide for Small Groups

The following plans outline nineteen study sessions, each lasting an hour to an hour and a half. These can easily be combined for groups preferring to meet for longer blocks of time or in a retreat setting. The arrangement of the stories allows for selection of those most relevant to the needs of the group. You will probably want to include the "Toolbox" pages, which present effective relationship skills and principles, even if you omit the particular stories to which they are linked.

You may wish to incorporate into all or some of the sessions the following four-step devotional approach to Scripture, which is based on the ancient Benedictine practice of *lectio divina*, as presented in *Gathered in the Word: Praying the Scripture in Small Groups* (pages 17–18).

1. Invite participants to settle comfortably in their chairs and close their eyes, breathing deeply to quiet and focus their minds. Instruct them to listen for a word that attracts their attention as you read a Scripture passage linked to the story or commentary. Read the passage twice. After a moment of silence, invite participants to record their words in their journals and/or to speak them aloud.
2. Invite the group to listen quietly while another member reads the same passage aloud and then to ponder how that passage touches their lives. After a moment of silence, invite participants to record their thoughts in their journals and/or to share them with the group.
3. Invite the group to listen quietly while yet another member reads the passage, this time reflecting on what the passage seems to be suggesting that they do or be during the next few days. Again, after a moment of silence, invite participants to share their thoughts or record them in their journals.
4. Close with a prayer circle, in which each member prays for empowerment of the person on his or her right to do or to be whatever the Scripture passage has suggested.

Appropriate hymns for use with this study include the following. Numbers given are for *The United Methodist Hymnal,* but many of these may be found in other books, along with other hymns of love and faith.
Amazing Grace, 378
Blest Be the Tie That Binds, 557
Great Is Thy Faithfulness, 140
Happy the Home When God Is There, 445

How Firm a Foundation, 529
O Perfect Love, 645
Savior, Like a Shepherd Lead Us, 381
The Gift of Love, 408
When Love Is Found, 643
Where Charity and Love Prevail, 549

SESSION ONE: INTRODUCTION

Goal: Participants will become better acquainted with other people in the group and gain appreciation for the importance of building strong, healthy marriage relationships.

Preparation: Read quickly through the entire book, considering whether you want to use all of it or selected stories only. More carefully read the "Introduction" (pages 5–6) and this session outline. Set up chairs in a circle, with open space facing a chalkboard or newsprint chart. Prepare a worship center, with a prayer candle to symbolize the sacred nature of this study, an open Bible to indicate its grounding in God's Word, and a plant to represent personal and relational growth. You might also include a wedding portrait, a statuette of a couple embracing, or a replica of Noah's ark.

Supplies: Nametag materials, a copy of this book for each person or couple, newsprint charts, pens, and items for the worship center (as suggested above). Each participant should bring a small notebook for journaling while preparing assignments and during some of the group sessions. You may want to provide extra notebooks and pens or pencils for those who forget to bring them.

Session Outline

1. Greet and welcome each individual, updating your attendance list and making sure you have correct addresses and telephone numbers. Introduce participants to each other, providing nametag materials if members do not already know each other well.

2. Introduce yourself and light the prayer candle, offering a brief prayer of thanks for this learning opportunity and for the blessings to be shared in this study, perhaps recalling Jesus' promise: "For where two or three are gathered in my name, I am there among them" (Matthew 18:20).

3. State the purpose of the study, either by reading aloud the "Introduction" (pages 5–6) or by expressing that information in your own words. Conclude by reading Hebrews 11:7a.

4. Ask the following questions: "What did you learn from your family of origin about marriage?" "What was helpful, and what have you had to unlearn?" If you have singles in your group, add this variation: "If you are not married, what do you think was helpful, and what do you think you might need to unlearn?" If your group consists entirely of couples, invite them to talk privately with each other in response to the questions. Otherwise, divide into small clusters of three or four people for discussion. If you have enough time, encourage more personal reflection by giving five minutes or so for individuals to write responses in their journals before sharing with their spouse or small group. Remind groups to give everyone a chance to speak. After ten minutes or so, ask someone from each small group to report to the large group some of what was shared.

5. Invite the group to brainstorm with you a list of the "Tasks of Marriage" by asking this question: "What are the tasks that married couples must accomplish in order to build a strong and healthy relationship?" Receive without judgment and record on newsprint all responses. Suggestions might include the following: adjust to different likes and dislikes, preferences, and habits; shift from a purely individual identity to a couple identity; adapt to the imperfections and peculiarities of one's mate and marriage; establish and furnish a home; learn to balance education, career, and family life; make decisions about family planning and parenting; negotiate household responsibilities; renegotiate relationships with family members and in-laws. (From a Smart Marriages/Happy Families Conference presentation, July 1998, by Dennis Lowe and Emily Scott-Lowe, Center for the Family, Pepperdine University. Used by permission.) Be sure to include preparation for dealing with hardships.

6. When all the ideas of the group have been listed, point back to the item or items related to preparation for dealing with hardships and ask, "What can married couples do to equip themselves to face and deal with whatever hardships befall them? How can a marriage serve, like Noah's ark, to keep us afloat in high-water, troubled times?" According to the amount of time you have available, allow for individual journaling, couple or small-group sharing, and/or whole-group discussion or brainstorming in response to these questions. Responses could be listed on newsprint under the heading "Preparing for Difficult Times."

7. Ask whether anyone in the group has participated in effective marriage preparation programs, marriage enrichment, Marriage

Encounter, or other marital-growth programs. Invite them to share what they learned through those experiences about building strong, healthy relationships.

8. Read the following statement: "Marriage preparation and marital-growth programs are an essential part of a church's ministry, but there are some particularly difficult situations couples may face that require extraordinary faith and commitment, as well as special support and understanding from others. This study will address five such situations: responding to family crises and concerns, living separately or traveling frequently because of career demands, healing wounded relationships, supporting a spouse through illness, and facing death."

9. Assignment: Ask everyone to read the assignment for the next session, underlining comments or feelings to which they can relate, and making a check mark beside anything they would like the group to discuss. Couples sharing a book could use different-colored pens for these markings. Encourage participants to journal in response to the "Reflection" questions. If stories are to be read aloud in the group setting, participants could follow along, marking the text at the same time.

10. Closing prayer: "Loving Creator, we thank you for the gift of love and for the institution of marriage as a crucible for nurturing and refining love. We thank you for our families of origin and for the families in which we now live by your grace. Help us to do your will, so loving each other that we may face whatever difficulties come our way and that we may bless the wider circles of which we are a part. In Jesus' name. Amen."

SESSIONS TWO THROUGH NINETEEN

1. **Preparation:** Read the assignment yourself, marking passages (as indicated above) and journaling in response to the "Reflection" questions. Read the "Additional Activities" given in this leader's guide for the upcoming session and make any particular preparation as indicated. Be sure to have newsprint and pens available for any brainstorming activities. Set up chairs and a worship center (as described above), and welcome participants, offering nametags again, if needed. You might invite a volunteer to light the prayer candle and offer a brief opening prayer.

2. **Discussion:** Invite participants to share what they underlined or marked for discussion in the material they read for this session and to share responses to the "Reflection" questions, either before or after

the specific activities listed for that session. If your group is large and time permits, allow discussion by couples or small groups, followed by reporting to the whole group.

3. **Additional Activities:** These are given for each session.
4. **Bible Study:** A process is suggested on pages 103–4.
5. **Reading Assignment:** Assign pages to be read before the next session, with directions for underlining, marking, and journaling, as suggested in Step 9 of Session One (page 106).
6. **Closing Prayer:** Give thanks for the couple who told their story and for the particular insights of the session. Pray God's blessing for participants as they face the challenges of the coming week.

SESSION TWO

Reading: "Commentary: Our Mutual Burdens Bear" (page 7) and "His Eye Is on the Sparrow" (pages 8–12)

Goal: Participants will consider how faith and supportive community can help a family cope with traumatic events.

Additional Activity: Encourage personal storytelling in response to the first two "Reflection" questions.

SESSION THREE

Reading: "Choosing to Be Blessed" (pages 13–17)

Goal: Participants will consider the particular needs of families dealing with chronic illness.

Preparation: Find out what support groups are available in your community for parents dealing with chronically ill children. Obtain literature from such groups and find out what kinds of help they offer.

Additional Activities

1. Share information about support groups and help available in your community.
2. List families in your church and community who are dealing with chronically ill children. Include them in your prayers, and plan ways to minister to them more effectively.

SESSION FOUR

Reading: "Stitches in the Fabric of Our Love" (pages 18–21) and "Toolbox: Communicating Feelings" (page 97)

Goal: Participants will learn about "tough love" for dealing with drug-addicted children, about the need for couples to be together in their parenting, and about the importance of sharing feelings.

Preparation

1. Invite someone who has participated in Marriage Encounter to tell about that experience and/or ask participants to read books on communicating feelings, such as *A Lasting Promise* (pages 50–57).

2. With your spouse or another member of the group, prepare a demonstration of "I-messages" and "active listening" (as described below), or invite another couple to do so.

Additional Activities

1. If you have people in your group who have participated in Marriage Encounter, or if you know someone who would be willing, invite them to share what that experience has meant to them.

2. After discussing the first three "Reflection" questions, brainstorm a list of feelings. Write the participants' responses on newsprint or on a chalkboard, without evaluation or comment. Be sure to include both positive and negative feelings on the list. Ask participants to note which feelings are easiest to express and which are most difficult.

3. Demonstrate "I-messages" and "active listening," as described below and in "Toolbox: Communicating Feelings" (page 97), and then allow group members an opportunity to practice. You might enlist volunteers to model this process before the group, but be prepared to coach them if they have not practiced this skill before. Following demonstrations, participants could be given the opportunity to practice this process in pairs or in small groups. Remind participants that for most people, unless they grew up in families that accepted feelings and communicated effectively, learning this process takes a lot of practice. Intentionally incorporate such practice into future group sessions.

   Directions: Pick one of the feelings that you have experienced or are experiencing now. Express that feeling by saying, "I feel…" and naming the feeling. The listener is to respond, "Tell me about it," and then listen carefully while the speaker proceeds to briefly describe the circumstances as objectively as possible, without assigning blame. When the speaker has finished, the listener should repeat what he or she has heard, focusing in on underlying feelings, if possible. No attempt should be made to solve problems at this point; that comes later.

SESSION FIVE

Reading: "Caregiving Together" (pages 22–26) and "Toolbox: Negotiating Solutions" (page 98)

Goal: Participants will consider issues related to caring for elderly parents and learn an effective way to negotiate solutions to problems.

Preparation: Read pages 59–69 in *A Lasting Promise* or other material about negotiating solutions to conflicts. Prepare a demonstration, or invite someone who has experience with this technique to demonstrate it for the group.

Additional Activities

1. While discussing the second "Reflection" question, encourage sharing of personal experiences with eldercare. Ask how many of your participants consider themselves part of the "sandwich generation," trying to care for parents and children at the same time. Invite them to share how they experience the pressure of juggling these roles and what strategies they have found helpful for keeping their balance and for maintaining vital, healthy marriages.

2. Invite participants to journal and share in regard to unresolved conflicts with their parents and how these either have complicated decision-making or might surface as their parents become more dependent on them. Encourage use of the process in "Toolbox: Communicating Feelings" (page 97), as practiced in the last session.

3. Review "Toolbox: Negotiating Solutions" (page 98), modeling the process and allowing participants to practice with such issues as "How will we spend our vacation?" or "How can we more fairly divide household chores?"

SESSION SIX

Reading: "Commentary: Not Bound by Space and Time" (page 27), "Life Is Change; Growth Is Optional" (pages 28–31), and "Toolbox: Two Ways to Improve a Marriage" (page 99)

Goal: Participants will discuss ways to deal with separation and will also discuss the difference between marriage enrichment experiences and counseling.

Additional Activities

1. Before discussion, brainstorm a list of reasons why couples might choose or have to live apart for a period of time. (Brainstorming involves the whole group in responding to the question. Responses should be recorded on newsprint or on a chalkboard, without evaluation.) Ask participants if they or any couples they know have had this experience.

2. Before discussing the second "Reflection" question, if you have not already covered the information in "Toolbox: Two Ways to Improve a Marriage" (page 99), ask two group members to read aloud the matching items, one at a time, first from the "Enrichment" list and

then from the "Counseling" list, to dramatize the contrasts between them. To encourage additional discussion of the second question, ask the following: "What attitudes toward counseling were expressed in your family of origin? Have there been any changes in those attitudes? Would you be comfortable telling your family that you were seeing a counselor? Would you be comfortable telling your church family? Do you think less of others who seek help through counseling?"

3. If group members have participated in marriage enrichment events or in counseling, this might be a good time for them to share what they gained from those experiences, if they are willing. Discuss criteria people might use for choosing a counselor or therapist

SESSION SEVEN

Reading: "Frequent Flyers" (pages 32–36) and "Toolbox: Managing Anger" (page 100)

Goal: Participants will reflect on the stress caused by frequent separations and on ways to manage anger as a tool for growth.

Additional Activity: After discussing the "Reflection" questions and the information in "Toolbox: Managing Anger," invite participants to journal and/or discuss these additional questions: What did you learn about anger when you were growing up? How do you usually behave when you are angry? What is the result of this behavior? What would you like to learn to do differently? What might help you to do that?

SESSION EIGHT

Reading: "Leap of Faith" (pages 37–40) and "Toolbox: Nurturing Spiritual Growth" (page 101)

Goal: Participants will reflect on the particular difficulties of a couple from a country at war and on ways to nurture spiritual growth.

Additional Activity: After discussion, encourage participants to reflect on their own spirituality and spiritual practices, considering how they might like to grow in this area. Invite them to journal, share in small groups, or discuss in the large group, depending on the time available and the comfort level of the group.

SESSION NINE

Reading: "Commentary: Love's Easter Song" (page 41) and "Repairing the Foundation" (pages 42–46)

Goal: Participants will reflect on what it means to make one's spouse a real priority, not just an intended one.

Preparation: Gather a jar and enough rocks of various sizes for the demonstration described below.

Additional Activities

1. Before discussing the "Reflection" questions, set an empty jar on a table in front of the group, with the largest rocks beside it. Ask the group to guess how many of the rocks will fit into the jar. Place the rocks in the jar until they reach the top of the jar; then ask the group if the jar is full yet. Next bring out some smaller rocks and pour them into the jar, filling in the spaces around the larger rocks. Ask again if the jar is full. Then bring out some sand and, finally, some water, pouring into the jar as much of each as you can. Ask the group what point has been made by the demonstration. After some discussion, if no one has stated the following, the presenter should say, "If the big rocks don't go in the jar first, they won't fit into the jar at all. Our priorities are like that. The big rocks represent our 'intended priorities'—but if they don't get put in the jar first, they will not be our 'actual priorities.'" (This demonstration is described in *First Things First: To Live, to Love, to Learn, to Leave a Legacy,* pages 88–89.)

2. Ask the participants to list in their journals their "intended" priorities. Then invite them to list their "actual" priorities, based on the way they spend their time and energy.

SESSION TEN

Reading: "Restoring Our Love" (pages 47–52)

Goal: Participants will consider the disappointment that may result when premarital expectations are not realized and will learn how one couple's relationship was healed through Retrouvaille.

Additional Activity: Brainstorm a list of issues that create conflict in marriage. Choose one or more and practice the process described in "Toolbox: Negotiating Solutions" (page 98), either as roleplays or with issues that are real for the participants. Coaching support can be provided by having two couples work together, one working on an issue and the other reminding them of the process when necessary, without getting drawn into the discussion. Make yourself available to provide additional coaching as needed.

SESSION ELEVEN

Reading: "To Heal the Hurt" (pages 53–56) and "Toolbox: Nurturing and Protecting Your Love" (page 102)

Goal: Participants will learn how committed Christians helped a couple work through a crisis involving infidelity and will consider how to protect marriages from the seduction of other attractions.

Additional Activity: Invite participants to discuss plans couples could make for dealing with extra-marital attractions.

SESSION TWELVE

Reading: "Behind Our Masks" (pages 57–60)

Goal: Participants will deepen their understanding of intimacy and consider ways to increase intimacy in their relationships.

Additional Activities

1. After discussion, invite participants to share how they experience some of the different kinds of intimacy listed in the second "Reflection" question.
2. Invite participants to journal (and share with their spouses, if this is a couples group) one or more kinds of intimacy they would like to increase in their relationships and then to brainstorm some things they could do to help this to happen.

SESSION THIRTEEN

Reading: "Choosing to Love and Forgive" (pages 61–64)

Goal: Participants will consider the power of forgiveness in healing broken relationships.

Additional Activity: After discussion, invite participants to journal and/or to tell about specific behaviors that strengthen relationships.

SESSION FOURTEEN

Reading: "Commentary: In Sickness and in Health" (page 65) and "An Unexpected Challenge" (pages 66–69)

Goal: Participants will consider how couples may cope when one of them has a serious illness.

Preparation: Locate a guided meditation, either on tape or one you can read. See pages 227–35 in *Love, Medicine, and Miracles*, by Bernie

Siegel, or pages 138–40 in *Getting Well Again*, by O. Carl Simonton, Stephanie Matthews-Simonton, and James L. Creighton.

Additional Activities

1. After discussion, invite participants to journal in response to the following sentence-starter: "If faced with a serious illness or life-threatening injury, my own or my spouse's, I hope that...." Responses may be shared in pairs or small groups, as time permits.
2. Lead participants in the guided meditation you have prepared.

SESSION FIFTEEN

Reading: "The 'Dis-ease' of a Disease" (pages 70–72)

Goal: Participants will continue discussion about coping with serious illness, with special focus on experiencing grace.

Preparation: Look up the word *grace* in a Bible dictionary or other resource book, or ask several pastors or other church leaders to explain its meaning.

Additional Activities

1. Before discussing the "Reflection" questions, explain the definitions of *grace* you have found. Ask the group for any other definitions or explanations they may want to express.
2. After the discussion, revisit "Toolbox: Communicating Feelings" (page 97). Invite participants to share experiences of using these skills effectively and/or provide opportunities to practice them, as described in Session Four (page 108).

SESSION SIXTEEN

Reading: "Intervention" (pages 73–77)

Goal: Participants will discuss issues related to the disease of alcoholism.

Preparation: Obtain information on alcoholism from your local Alcoholics Anonymous or Al-Anon groups, which are listed in the classified section of newspapers, or invite someone familiar with the topic to share in this session.

Additional Activity: Before discussing the "Reflection" questions, provide information about alcoholism as a disease, either from your own reading and experience or by inviting a guest speaker.

SESSION SEVENTEEN

Reading: "A Walking, Talking Miracle" (pages 78–82)

Goal: Participants will share in the experience of a family involved in a serious accident and reflect on the healing power of intercessory prayer.

Preparation: Locate recent news articles that report research on the power of prayer. One possible resource is *Healing Words: The Power of Prayer and the Practice of Medicine*, by Larry Dossey, M.D.

Additional Activities

1. After discussion, share and discuss the research reports you found.
2. Invite participants to participate in a time of intercessory prayer, offering up names of people who are dealing with serious illness or injury. After each name is lifted up, the whole group may respond by saying, "Lord, in your mercy, hear our prayer." Conclude with a prayer for whatever healing is needed by group members.
3. Invite the group to consider how they might be supportive to any of those they have prayed for, either individually or as a group, and then allow a few minutes for planning.

SESSION EIGHTEEN

Reading: "To Comprehend a Nectar" (pages 83–86)

Goal: Participants will consider healing, in the broadest sense.

Preparation: Find and look through healing services, such as those in *The United Methodist Book of Worship* (pages 613–29).

Additional Activities

1. Before discussion, ask whether any of the group members have ever participated in healing services. Show them the variety available in *The United Methodist Book of Worship* or other resources you have found.
2. After discussion, invite participants to journal in regard to concrete changes for improving their health, happiness, and relationships, fantasizing how they would like to be a year from now.
3. Invite participants to select one or more specific steps they could take during the next week to work toward this change and to write a brief contract indicating what they will do, when, and where.
4. Invite participants to consider what support they will need in order to implement these steps. (Numbers 2, 3, and 4 are based on a process described in Wayne and Mary Sotile's *Supercouple Syndrome*, pages 141–60.)

5. Allow time for couples or the whole group to share their plans. In the closing prayer, name each participant, invoking God's grace and the power of the Holy Spirit for actualizing each one's intentions.
6. If time allows, conduct a healing service, like that in *The United Methodist Book of Worship* (pages 622–23), or you could plan to use such a service at the conclusion of the next session.

SESSION NINETEEN

Reading: "Commentary: Until We Are Parted by Death" (page 87) and "Life Quake" (pages 88–95)

Goal: Participants will explore attitudes toward death and ways to prepare for it.

Additional Activities

1. After discussion, revisit the contracts participants wrote during the last session. Celebrate with those who report having lived up to their intention. Affirm God's grace for those who did not.
2. Invite participants to reflect on long- and short-term goals for themselves and their relationships. If you have a couples group, suggest listing goals under the following three headings: "What I Want for Me," "What I Want for You," "What I Want for Us."
3. Encourage participants to pick one or two items related to these goals and contract to implement them within a reasonable time frame.
4. If there is interest, make plans to meet for a follow-up session or to function as an ongoing support group for a specific period of time.
5. Evaluate this group experience by asking participants to list for you what has been most helpful and what they would suggest doing differently another time.
6. If this is your final group session, close with an appropriate ritual, such as a prayer circle in which each person gives thanks for and asks blessings for the person to his or her right; a healing service; Communion; renewal of wedding vows; or commitment ceremony for ministry to married couples.

Sources

A Lasting Promise: A Christian Guide to Fighting for Your Marriage, by Scott Stanley, Daniel Trathen, Savanna McCain, and Milt Bryan (San Francisco: Jossey-Bass Publishers, 1998).

An Affair of the Mind: One Woman's Courageous Battle to Salvage Her Family From the Devastation of Pornography, by Laurie Hall (Colorado Springs: Focus on the Family Publishing, 1996).

"Enrichment and Counseling—Two Ways to Improve a Marriage," by Antoinette and Leon Smith, in *The Association for Couples in Marriage Enrichment Newsletter*, Volume 17, Number 7, July–August 1989.

First Things First: To Live, to Love, to Learn, to Leave a Legacy, by Stephen R. Covey, A. Roger Merrill, and Rebecca R. Merrill (New York: Simon and Schuster, 1994).

Gathered in the Word: Praying the Scripture in Small Groups, by Norvene Vest (Nashville: Upper Room Books, 1996).

Getting Well Again: A Step-by-Step, Self-Help Guide to Overcoming Cancer for Patients and Their Families, by O. Carl Simonton, M.D., Stephanie Matthews-Simonton, and James L. Creighton (New York: Bantam Books, Inc., 1978).

Healing Words: The Power of Prayer and the Practice of Medicine, by Larry Dossey, M.D. (New York: HarperCollins Publishers, 1993).

Heart Illness and Intimacy: How Caring Relationships Aid Recovery, by Wayne M. Sotile, Ph.D. (Baltimore: The Johns Hopkins University Press, 1992).

How to Have a Happy Marriage: A Step-by-Step Guide to an Enriched Relationship, by David and Vera Mace (Nashville: Abingdon Press, 1977).

Jonathan Livingston Seagull: A Story, by Richard Bach (New York: Avon Books, 1970).

Love and Anger in Marriage, by David Mace (Grand Rapids, MI: Zondervan Publishing House, 1982).

Love Life for Every Married Couple: How to Fall in Love, Stay in Love, Rekindle Your Love, by Ed Wheat, M.D., and Gloria Okes Perkins (New York: HarperCollins Publishers, 1980).

Love, Medicine, and Miracles: Lessons Learned About Self-Healing From a Surgeon's Experience With Exceptional Patients, by Bernie S. Siegel, M.D. (New York: Harper & Row, Publishers, 1986).

Parent Effectiveness Training: The "No-Lose" Program for Raising Responsible Children, by Dr. Thomas Gordon (New York: Peter H. Wyden, Inc., 1970).

Rekindled, by Pat and Jill Williams, with Jerry Jenkins (Tarrytown, NY: Fleming H. Revell Company, 1985).

Supercouple Syndrome: How Overworked Couples Can Beat Stress Together, by Wayne M. Sotile, Ph.D., and Mary O. Sotile, M.A (New York: John Wiley & Sons, Inc., 1998).

Team Spirituality: A Guide for Staff and Church, by William J. Carter (Nashville: Abingdon Press, 1997).

The Dance of Anger: A Woman's Guide to Changing the Patterns of Intimate Relationships, by Harriet Goldhor Lerner, Ph.D. (New York: Harper & Row, Publishers, 1985).

The Heart of Commitment, by Scott Stanley, Ph.D. (Nashville: Thomas Nelson Publishers, 1998).

The Intimate Marriage, by Howard J. Clinebell, Jr., and Charlotte H. Clinebell (New York: Harper & Row, Publishers, 1970).

The Life Recovery Bible (The Living Bible) (Wheaton, IL: Tyndale House Publishers, Inc., 1992).

The Relaxation Response, by Herbert Benson, M.D. (New York: Avon Books, 1975).

The Twelve Steps for Christians, Revised Edition (Julian, CA: RPI Publishing, Inc., 1994).

The United Methodist Book of Worship (Nashville: The United Methodist Publishing House, 1992).

The United Methodist Hymnal (Nashville: The United Methodist Publishing House, 1989).

When Bad Things Happen to Good People, by Harold S. Kushner (New York: Schocken Books, 1981).

Resources for Further Help

Association for Couples in Marriage Enrichment (A.C.M.E.). This international organization provides training and certification for leader couples, activities (retreats, conferences, and other events), and resources for building marriages that are strong and satisfying to both partners. Address: A.C.M.E., P.O. Box 10596, Winston-Salem, NC 27108. Phone: 800-634-8325. E-mail: ACME@marriageenrichment.com Internet: **http://www.marriageenrichment.com**

Center for the Family at Pepperdine University. Dennis Lowe, Ph.D, Emily Scott-Lowe, Ph.D., and Sara Jackson, M.A., offer training for marriage mentoring and other marriage and family enrichment programs. Address: Center for the Family, 24255 Pacific Coast Highway, Malibu, CA 90263-4771. Phone: 310-456-4771. E-mail: sjackson@pepperdine.edu or dlowe@pepperdine.edu Internet: **http://www.pepperdine.edu/gsep/family**

Coalition for Marriage, Family, and Couples Education, LLC (CMFCE). This website offers discussion and articles on marriage education issues and a directory of available courses for couples. Internet: **http://www.smartmarriages.com**

Couple Relationships. Offers information about marriage education. Internet: **http://www.uwyo.edu/ag/ces/family/relationships.htm**

Do-It-Yourself Marriage Enrichment: A Workshop on Your Own Time, on Your Own Terms, on Your Own Turf, by Warren and Mary Ebinger (Nashville: Abingdon Press, 1998). This book provides helpful suggestions and exercises for couples to use on their own—on their own time and at their own pace. Material could also be used in groups. Phone: 800-672-1789.

Dr. Pat Love and Associates. Training and resources for "Hot Monogamy," "IMAGO," and other personal-growth and relationship workshops. Address: Pat Love and Associates, PMB 291, 6705 Highway 290 West, Suite 502, Austin, TX 78735. Phone: 512-891-0610. E-mail:pat@patlove.com   Internet: **http://www.patlove.com**

Marriage Alive International, Inc. Claudia and David Arp, M.S.S.W., present seminars and programs, as well as offering a variety of books, video curriculum, program materials, and online services. Books include *The Second Half of Marriage: Facing the Eight Challenges of Every Long-Term Marriage* (1998); *10 Great Dates to Revitalize Your Marriage: The Best Tips From the Marriage Alive! Seminars* (1997); *Marriage Moments: Heart-to-Heart Times to Deepen Your Love* (1998); and *Love Life for Parents: How to Have Kids and a Sex Life Too* (1998). Phone: 888-690-6667. E-mail: mace@marriagealive.com Internet: **http://www.marriagealive.com**

Marriage Ministry. A Christian, church-based, couple-to-couple program of Christian Healing Ministry, Inc., for divorce prevention. Address: P.O. Box 9520, Jacksonville, FL 32208. Phone: 904-765-3332.

Marriage Savers. This national organization offers resources to aid churches in training mentoring couples to help other couples avoid bad marriages, strengthen existing marriages, and save troubled marriages. Their resources include:

- *Marriage Savers: Helping Your Friends and Family Avoid Divorce,* by Michael J. McManus (Grand Rapids, MI: Zondervan Publishing House, 1995). This book reviews theories and practices related to Community Marriage Covenants and marriage-support programs.
- *Marriage Savers Resource Collection.* Includes six videos, two books— *Marriage Savers: Helping Your Friends and Family Avoid Divorce* (1995) and *Insuring Marriage: 25 Proven Ways to Prevent Divorce* (1996)—and a 13-session leader's guide. $150.00 plus $8.00 shipping and handling.

Address: Marriage Savers, Inc., 9311 Harrington Drive, Potomac, MD 20854. Phone: 301-469-5873. E-mail: mikemcmanus@marriagesavers.org Internet: **http://www.marriagesavers.org**

PREP (Prevention and Relationship Enhancement Program). Howard Markman, Ph.D., Scott Stanley, Ph.D., Susan Blumberg, Ph.D., and others offer research-based programs, training, and resources. Among their titles are *Fighting for Your Marriage: Positive Steps for Preventing Divorce and Preserving a Lasting Love* (1996); *A Lasting Promise: A Christian Guide to Fighting for Your Marriage* (1998); and *We Can Work it Out: How to Solve Conflicts, Save Your Marriage, and Strengthen Your Love for Each Other* (1994). Address: PREP, Inc., P.O. Box 102530, Denver, CO 80250-2530. Phone: 303-759-9931 (ext. 932) or 800-366-0166. Fax: 303-759-4212. E-mail: prepinc@aol.com Internet: **http://members.aol.com/prepinc**

REFOCCUS (Relationship Enrichment Facilitating Open Couple Communication). A marriage enrichment tool by B. Markey, M. Micheletto, and A. Becker for use by couples or within a group (with or without a facilitator). Provides concrete means for strengthening relationships. Five areas for discussion: Marriage as a Process, Intimacy, Compatibility, Communication, Commitment. Address: Family Life Office, Archdiocese of Omaha, 3214 North 60th St., Omaha, NE 68104-3495. Phone: 402-551-9003. Fax: 402-551-3050.

Retrouvaille (Rediscovery: A Lifeline for Troubled Marriages). This Roman Catholic program, which is open to all faiths, includes a weekend session and six follow-up sessions. It is designed to help heal and renew couples who are drifting—or have drifted—apart. Phone: 800-470-2230. Internet: **http://www.retrouvaille.org**

Smalley Relationship Center. Gary Smalley offers books, seminars, and video programs, including *Making Love Last Forever, Love Is a Decision*, and *Hidden Keys to a Loving, Lasting Relationship*. Address: 1482 Lakeshore Drive, Branson, MO 65616. Phone: 800-848-6329. E-mail: family@smalleyrelationships.com Internet: **http://www.smalleyrelationships.com**

Vaughan-Vaughan.com. This website features books by Peggy and James Vaughan (including *Beyond Affairs, The Monogamy Myth*, and *Making Love Stay*) and workshops for dealing with extra-marital affairs and for balancing work and family life. Internet: **http://www.vaughan-vaughan.com**

Worldwide Marriage Encounter. This weekend experience, designed for couples who have good marriages and want to make them even better, focuses on communication between husbands and wives. Address: Worldwide Marriage Encounter, 2210 East Highland Ave., Suite 106, San Bernadino, CA 92404-4666. Phone: 909-863-9963 or 800-795-5683. Internet (Worldwide): **http://www.wwme.org** Internet (United Methodist): **http://www.encounter.org**

FOR DEALING WITH DEATH AND DYING

Our Greatest Gift: A Meditation on Dying and Caring, by Henri J. M. Nouwen (New York: HarperCollins Publishers, 1994).

The Grace in Dying: How We Are Transformed Spiritually as We Die, by Kathleen Dowling Singh (New York: HarperSanFrancisco, 1998).